The Impact of Identity in K–8 Mathematics Learning and Teaching:
Rethinking Equity-Based Practices

Julia Maria Aguirre
University of Washington–Tacoma

Karen Mayfield-Ingram
University of California, Berkeley

Danny Bernard Martin
University of Illinois at Chicago

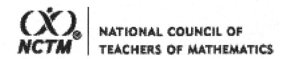

NATIONAL COUNCIL OF
TEACHERS OF MATHEMATICS

more4u
www.nctm.org/more4u
Access code: ILT14119

Copyright © 2013 by
The National Council of Teachers of Mathematics, Inc.
1906 Association Drive, Reston, VA 20191-1502
(703) 620-9840; (800) 235-7566; www.nctm.org
All rights reserved
Tenth printing 2021

Library of Congress Cataloging-in-Publication Data

Martin, Danny Bernard.
  The impact of identity in K–8 mathematics teaching : rethinking equity-based practices / Danny Bernard Martin, University of Illinois at Chicago, Julia Aguirre, University of Washington–Tacoma, Karen Mayfield-Ingram, Lawrence Hall of Science, Berkeley, California.
     pages cm
  Includes bibliographical references.
  ISBN 978-0-87353-689-9
  1. Mathematics--Study and teaching (Elementary)--United States. 2.Educational equalization--United States. I. Aguirre, Julia. II.Mayfield-Ingram, Karen. III. Title.
  QA13.M454 2013
  372.7--dc23

2012048405

The National Council of Teachers of Mathematics advocates for
high-quality mathematics teaching and learning for each and every student.

Printed in the United States of America

Contents

Accompanying Materials at More4U

Chapter 3
Mathematics Learning Autobiography

Teacher Identity Activity

Chapter 4
Midway Suspensions (Lesson 1)

Two Sides to Every Story (Lesson 2)

Chapter 5
Multiplication Stations Lesson

Chapter 7
Parent-Teacher Conference Template

Preface

The increasingly political environment of educational reform—motivated by concerns about U.S. students' lagging performance on international comparisons, the push for national learning standards, and stricter accountability measures—has subjected mathematics teachers and mathematics teaching practice to intense scrutiny by policymakers, educational researchers, and much of the general public.

In one way or another, teachers are being told that they are responsible for the poor mathematics performance of students. They are made to feel this responsibility on the local level, for students' performance in schools, and on national and international levels, for the perceived drop in U.S. international competitiveness. They are being told that they lack the requisite mathematics content knowledge to teach students effectively. For many teachers, determinations of their effectiveness and the quality of their teaching have now become solely dependent on whether they can raise their students' test scores.

Much of the discourse generated about teachers and teacher practice has been top-down, focused primarily on curriculum and content, and generated by voices far from the classroom. Often absent from this discourse are teachers' own reflections on their work and the demands placed on them. Teaching is complex professional work that requires ongoing reflection on curriculum and content, as well as self-reflection— reflection about children and families, reflection about the role of mathematics in the lives of children and families, and even reflection about routine, everyday practice.

This book focuses on teacher reflection. Our goal is not to generate discourse *about* teachers. Instead, it is to engage in conversations *with* teachers, raising issues that we have seen in our individual and collective classroom experiences and that many teachers will recognize from their own experiences.

We have chosen to focus on teacher reflection and practice in the context of mathematics learning and identity development. That is, we have chosen to focus on understanding how teachers help students become powerful learners of mathematics and how students come to see themselves in relationship to mathematics learning, both inside and outside the classroom. Our commitment to teacher reflection is grounded in our desire to help teachers understand, appreciate, and draw on the backgrounds of students as strengths to further students' mathematical development—especially those students who have not had eqitable access or opportunity to learn mathematics.

We acknowledge the dual role that mathematics has played as gatekeeper and gateway to various opportunities in society, and we recognize that mathematics has often been used to make judgments about intelligence. We call on teachers to reflect on these uses of mathematics. Further, because students do not come to school without the influences of their homes, communities, and cultures, we ask teachers to reflect on how the multiple identities that students are developing can influence their mathematics learning. Yet, we do not confine the conversation on mathematics learning to students. We ask teachers to reflect on their own learning experiences and how those experiences have shaped their senses of themselves as doers of mathematics and how their views of themselves as mathematics learners affect their classroom practice.

We also frame our conversation with teachers around issues of equity, focusing on fair and just treatment and a recognition of each child's needs that allows every child to develop as a powerful mathematics learner and affirms his or her intellectual, cultural, racial, ethnic, and linguistic background. The concerns for equity in this book also include fair and just treatment and recognition of teachers and the highly skilled activity of teaching. We respect and understand the critical roles that teachers play in helping students learn, as well as the constraints that often have an impact on their work.

This book, which consists of eight chapters divided into three parts, is designed to help teachers move beyond an awareness of the need to reflect on their teaching to a commitment to transform their teaching to include equity-based practices. An epilogue offers final reflections. A list of discussion questions appears at the end of each chapter to promote further dialogue and self-reflection. Readers can also use the access code on the title page to find specific reflection tools and activities at NCTM's More4U website (www.nctm.org/more4u).

Part 1 focuses on mathematics learning and identity. Chapter 1 addresses important themes related to the purposes of learning mathematics, equity, and shifts needed to attend to learning and identity. Chapter 2 discusses the connection between mathematics learning and student identity. This chapter discusses why teachers need to attend to this linkage to empower young mathematical minds. Chapter 3 shifts that identity focus to teachers, calling for reflection on the impact of one's own mathematics learning identity on instructional beliefs and classroom practice. Teacher identity is inextricably linked with instructional vision and practice, which in turn shape the mathematics experience of students.

Part 2 describes five equity-based instructional practices designed to strengthen mathematics learning and positive mathematics identity:

- Going deep with mathematics
- Leveraging multiple mathematical competencies
- Affirming mathematics learners' identities
- Challenging spaces of marginality
- Drawing on multiple resources of knowledge

The chapters in this part use classroom vignettes to bring these practices to life. Chapter 4 describes a middle school mathematics teacher's practice that cultivates mathematical agency and empowers students to examine claims by using mathematical evidence. Chapter 5 focuses on the way that an elementary teacher builds on students' strengths to foster their engagement with mathematics and thus support their learning of mathematics. Chapter 6 shines the spotlight on assessment. Drawing on the five equity practices, this chapter specifically discusses the role of meaningful feedback on typical classroom "tests"—feedback that can deepen students' learning and help develop their sense of themselves as mathematics learners. This discussion also highlights ways that teachers can learn to recognize various experiences and knowledge that students bring to bear on assessments and that demonstrate what they know and can do.

Part 3 focuses on the importance of engaging families and communities as true partners in supporting mathematics learning and positive mathematics identity development. Chapter 7 discusses routine strategies such as family newsletters and parent-teacher conferences, which can be enhanced to strengthen relationships with parents and effectively communicate the teacher's mathematics vision and the students' progress.

Chapter 8 moves beyond the classroom walls to highlight ways in which teachers and schools can partner with parents and communities to support mathematics learning and provide complementary resources to help children learn mathematics.

The epilogue offers final reflections about important ideas in the book and ways for teachers to continue deepening their equity-based practices to strengthen mathematics learning and positive mathematics identity development for children.

In writing this book, we have drawn on our own experiences in K–8 classrooms; our experiences with parents, teachers, and children; our experiences as teachers in various contexts and as teacher educators in preservice and in-service contexts; and, for two of us (Julia Aguirre and Karen Mayfield-Ingram), our experiences as parents of school-aged children. Each of us has a lifelong history of commitment to issues of equity in mathematics education, focusing on historically marginalized students and families. Our professional experiences and practices have been devoted to empowering students with mathematics to help them realize a full range of educational and life opportunities.

Our own journeys in mathematics, including being identified by teachers for accelerated tracks in mathematics, participating in academic enrichment programs for minorities and women, experiencing undergraduate and graduate study in mathematics and education, and being mentored in the areas of mathematics and mathematics education, have also shaped the writing of this book. We have known firsthand the impact of teachers on our lives in relation to mathematics learning.

Moreover, the writing of this book has been shaped by our own racial and cultural identities as well as the ways that we have come to see ourselves as learners and doers of mathematics as a result of those identities. Racially, ethnically, and culturally, for example, we self-identify with particular social categories (African American, Latina, multilingual, multiethnic, biracial) that have been marginalized in societal and school settings, especially with respect to mathematics. These social categories are both personal and political and have evolving histories and meanings, and we acknowledge the sociopolitical and power implications of these identifications.

We acknowledge that these categories and others—for instance, "white," "black," "Asian," and "Native American"—are negotiated, and each of us makes our own sense of what these terms mean and whether we choose to make them our own. We also acknowledge the shared history and experiences of group members despite different labels. For example, we use the labels "African American" and "black" to encompass the diverse ways that group members of the African diaspora self-identify and are identified by others. We use "Latina/o" as a pan-ethnic label to express the cultural and political solidarities of people who are descendants of or natives of a Western hemisphere country south of the United States, including Mexico and the countries of Central and South America and the Caribbean (Hurtado and Gurin 2004). "Latina/o" acknowledges Indigenous, African, and European ancestries that the label "Hispanic" does not. The categories "white" and "Asian" also include multiple identifications. In this book, we ask educators to recognize and critically reflect on how all of these terms are used in school discourses related to mathematics.

We hope that this book, in which we bring to bear our professional and personal experiences, will be an essential resource for teachers, teacher educators, and education researchers interested in teacher development, equity, learning, and identity. We trust that it will also prove useful to parents and school administrators who wish to support teachers in the teaching of mathematics. Most important, we hope that we have succeeded in shaping this book in such a way that it will push our collective thinking and practice to give our nation's youth a better preparation for learning mathematics and developing positive mathematics identities that will advance their own educational, career, and life opportunities. We hope that the examples presented in this book will resonate with teachers and provide opportunities for them to reflect critically on their beliefs and practices.

Acknowledgments

We are grateful for, and feel very fortunate to have been given, the opportunity to write this book. We owe a great deal of thanks to NCTM's Education Materials Committee. We are especially grateful to Myrna Jacobs, NCTM publications manager, for her patience and support for this project. We offer special thanks to our teacher colleagues Andy Coons, Desiree LeSage, Shelley Rafter, Susan Sabol, and Niral Shah for their insights, examples, and constructive critiques that helped us to think through some of the issues raised in this book. We would also like to thank our families for their ongoing support and inspiration.

We dedicate this book to all young students, past, present, and future, who continually teach us what is necessary to help them learn and grow mathematically and to the educators, families, and communities who, in the face of many challenges, demonstrate their dedication, love, and support for young people.

Part 1

Rethinking Mathematics Learning, Identity, and Equity

Focusing on the connection between mathematics learning and identity can help teachers reflect on their beliefs about students, mathematics learning, and equity. In part 1, first we ask teachers to reflect on the purposes of learning mathematics and the common perspectives that can lead students to develop positive and negative images of their mathematics competence. To spark discussion, we offer our definition of equity in mathematics education in relation to these issues. Next, we examine how a rich and complex view of students includes attention to the multiple identities that they are in the process of developing on the basis of their experiences in school and outside of school. We give particular attention to how these identities shape and are shaped by the students' mathematics identities and how teachers can leverage these identities to promote progress in mathematics, especially for traditionally marginalized students. Teachers are encouraged to reframe students' identities in ways that move beyond stereotypes and deficit views. We stress that students are active participants in their mathematics learning and should be encouraged to engage in multiple forms of mathematical agency.

Finally, we examine a variety of experiences that contribute to the development of what we call a "K–8 mathematics teacher identity." We present six case studies of new teachers, all of whom discuss their own experiences as learners of mathematics and aspects of their identities that were relevant in those experiences. K–8 mathematics teacher identities are also shaped by professional experiences and demands. Decisions and mandates about what content gets taught, to which students and by which teachers, shape mathematics identities for teachers and students. We give particular attention to mandates calling for "algebra for all," and how those mandates can challenge the identities of K–8 teachers.

Discussion questions at the end of each chapter provide an opportunity for teacher-readers to reflect on their own identities as well as the identities of their students. None of these identities are fixed or static. Deeper reflection will help teachers improve their own practice, and changes in their practice can help students develop more powerful mathematics identities. In the chapters that follow, all names of students, teachers, and schools in the vignettes and examples are pseudonyms unless otherwise noted.

Chapter 1

What Mathematics? For Whom? For What Purposes?

Throughout this book, we encourage all teachers to reflect on the three questions raised in this chapter's title: What mathematics? For whom? For what purposes? We raise these questions because they strike at the core of equity concerns in mathematics education and serve as reminders that school mathematics simultaneously serves as gateway and gatekeeper for various opportunities in and out of school. These opportunities include access to advanced courses, entrance to college, and access to math-dependent college majors and careers. Teachers play a crucial role in deciding which students will or will not have access to these opportunities.

Mathematics also provides a critical lens for discerning patterns and making sense of quantitative information that we experience in the world every day. However, some students are never given the opportunity to engage with mathematics in rich and meaningful ways that emphasize critical thinking and problem solving. Moreover, educators often use mathematics assessments to make definitive judgments about students' competencies and abilities. Such judgments can follow students throughout their academic careers and have a long-lasting impact on how they see themselves as doers of mathematics (Boaler 2002, 2008; Jackson 2009; Martin 2000, 2009; Spielhagen 2011).

We contend that deep, meaningful reflection on these questions will require teachers to examine their beliefs about learners, learning, and mathematics content, as well as their everyday teaching and classroom practices. This work also demands that teachers take a close look at their own mathematics learning experiences and how these shape their instructional vision and classroom practice. Furthermore, by thinking about how best to support students, teachers may need to reexamine their beliefs and retool their practices, not only to engage students more effectively in learning mathematics but also to partner more successfully with families and communities to support learning in and out of school.

This book provides examples, concepts, and reflective tools that teachers can use to build richer perspectives on issues of equity within the context of their routine, everyday classroom practices. Key to developing these richer perspectives and practices is attending to issues of identity and competence in relation to and through mathematics—that is, understanding who students are, who they are becoming, and who they want to become. It also means understanding how students are positioned as mathematics learners by what others—teachers, peers, or parents—say about who they are, such as who gets identified as "good at math" and who does not.

Consider the following vignette involving a young student, Baye, his father, and his mathematics teacher. The vignette highlights a number of issues related to student beliefs about mathematics, teacher practice and influence on those beliefs, and parental support for mathematics learning.

Baye is a third-generation Korean American sixth grader who is in his first year at Crestmont Middle School, located in a mid-sized city in the western United States. He is a rising star on the local track team and volunteers as a faith mentor for younger children at his local church. Although he has many leadership qualities and a strong preference for science, he struggles with learning mathematics.

Ms. Carlson is Baye's mathematics teacher. She believes strongly that all students can be successful in mathematics if given the right content and exposed to the right pedagogy. She recently transferred to Crestmont because it is one of the schools in the district that will be piloting curriculum units based on the new Common Core State Standards (National Governors Association Center for Best Practices and Council of Chief State School Officers 2010). In addition, Ms. Carlson believes in the added value of Crestmont's diverse student population. Crestmont is more ethnically and socioeconomically diverse than her previous middle school, Diablo Valley. Although Diablo Valley is a high-performing middle school, according to achievement test scores, Ms. Carlson was not as satisfied with the school's scores as her colleagues. She knew that many of the students had not developed the conceptual understanding to match their algorithmic mastery, and there were glaring disparities for some students. But whenever she voiced this concern to her colleagues, they told her that she was "creating issues."

Ms. Carlson was ready for a change. At Crestmont, she teaches Baye and twenty-two other sixth graders in a "support" math class designed to address the mathematics needs of struggling students. Ms. Carlson has the following exchange with Baye after assigning a mathematics task to her students:

Ms. Carlson:	Why haven't you gotten started, Baye?
Baye:	[*Whispers under his breath*] Because this is stupid. The problem makes no sense. Who cares how many different sizes the rabbits' playpen can be.
Ms. Carlson:	You haven't even tried the problem yet.
Baye:	[*Looks briefly at the students sitting around him and mumbles*] What difference does it make? I can't do it. That's why I'm in this class, right?

Before Ms. Carlson can answer, the bell rings, and Baye packs up and rushes out the door. Ms. Carlson reviews the class papers but can't get Baye out of her mind. "What am I going to do?" she wonders. "How do I get him to try? He seemed embarrassed when I was talking with him. How am I going to motivate these kids to want to learn math? How am I going to get them to believe they can do math?"

Later, at home that evening, Baye has the following encounter with his father:

Father:	How was school today?
Baye:	[*Shrugs*] OK, I guess.
Father:	Did you finish your homework after school? [*Pauses while Baye is silent.*] What's wrong?
Baye:	Nothing.

Baye throws his backpack on the table and heads outside. As his father takes the backpack off the table, he notices a crumpled piece of paper. It is a math assignment, but there is nothing on the page. He sighs and says to himself, "I thought this year would be different. He hates math. I don't know how to help. I didn't have any trouble with math in school. What am I going to do?"

From our experiences with students, teachers, and parents, we know that situations like the one involving Baye arise every day. We know that many teachers reflect deeply on these kinds of encounters with students. They are concerned about students feeling discouraged and frustrated by mathematics. They want to change the students' negative views of mathematics and of themselves as mathematics learners. We also know that many parents express similar concerns about their children in relation to mathematics. When their child is distressed, they want to help. In this case, both Ms. Carlson and Baye's father are concerned and desire to help. They are at a loss.

In contrast, we have frequently heard educators make statements like the following about particular students, their families, and mathematics learning: "My students come from impoverished backgrounds. They can't handle that kind of math." We have also heard race- and culture-based statements about black and Latina/o families "not valuing" their child's education, whereas white and Asian families supposedly "push their children" to do well in mathematics. Furthermore, some teachers question whether all children should study advanced levels of mathematics, echoing common public refrains like, "Not everybody needs to study algebra. They just need to know the basics," or "There should be other options for those who are less mathematically inclined," or "I didn't do so well in math, and I did just fine. I have a successful career."

Statements such as these are quite common yet may not accurately reflect students' identities, abilities, or interests. They are also not the most reflective, equity-oriented approaches that teachers can take. Moreover, these statements, although well intentioned, may actually perpetuate negative stereotypes about what mathematics is, who can learn mathematics, who supports mathematics, and why students should or should not pursue their studies of mathematics. In our view of equity-based practice, it is important to replace these viewpoints with alternative perspectives.

Beyond Changing Demographics

A common approach to engaging teachers about issues of equity is to broadly cite changing demographics and the increasing racial, ethnic, and linguistic diversity in the student population. However, such references do not always lead to the kind of deep reflection about practice that is necessary to strengthen mathematics learning and positive mathematics identity in students. We contend that although many teachers may be aware of and receptive to broad, general discussions of equity in mathematics, general awareness may not be enough to motivate them to address the particularities of working across and within particular student populations. In addition, focusing on demographic changes often positions students who are from different ethnic or language groups as at odds with dominant student groups. The students who are seen as diversifying the student population (often identified in racial, ethnic, or class terms) are frequently called on to conform to the established standards or norms. In our view, meaningful inclusion and interactions with students necessitate knowledge of their personal, family, and community backgrounds as well as their social realities. Gaining this knowledge may require additional effort on the part of teachers and administrators to fully meet the mathematical learning needs of their students.

For example, a few years ago, one of the authors, Danny Martin, gave a presentation at a regional conference of the National Council of Teachers of Mathematics (NCTM) in Chicago. In his presentation, he argued for the relevance of identity as a key consideration in the mathematical experiences of black children. In particular, Martin contended that teachers need to try to understand the ways in which these children make sense of what it means to be doers of mathematics, and, simultaneously, how they make sense of what it means to be black, on the basis of their own emerging understandings of their life experiences and social realities. He suggested that the emerging understandings developed by students reflect not only the assertions that students make about who they are but also the ways in which they accept or resist the racial and mathematical identities that are imposed on them by others, including teachers, peers, parents, community members, and the media.

In his presentation, Martin encouraged the audience, especially teachers, to think more deeply about these identity and learning issues by considering two focused questions:

1. What does it mean to be a learner and doer of mathematics in the context of being black?

2. What does it mean to be black in the context of learning and doing mathematics?

Martin asked teachers to consider the range of responses that might emerge among their own students, given their social realities, and how those responses might be useful to teachers as they reflect on their work with black children.

At the conclusion of Martin's talk, a young white female teacher in the audience raised her hand. She began her comments by noting that she was a teacher in a black school located in a black community on Chicago's South Side. She said that although she had been teaching at the school for a few years, she had "never thought about what it means for my students to be black." Martin's talk was a revelation to her as a teacher of black children.

We contend that it is reasonable to ask why this presentation was such a revelation to this teacher. How did this teacher's inattention to the power and relevance of black identity in the lives of her students evolve? And to what extent had her views up to this point affected her mathematics instruction in classrooms with black children? Although one could debate Martin's focus on black racial identity and its role in mathematics learning and teaching, attention to the local and larger contexts of this teacher's school and the children that she works with daily highlight its relevance. For example, the public school system in Chicago is the third largest in the United States, with black children making up more than 40 percent of the student population in the district. Chicago's public schools are, de facto, racially segregated, mirroring the racial separateness of the city's neighborhoods. The average black child attending a school in the district is in a school that is more than 80 percent black. Moreover, during the 2006–2007 school year—the year of Martin's presentation—thirty-one schoolchildren were murdered in Chicago, one per school week on average, and most of them black. Statistics such as these certainly make black racial identity socially significant and conspicuous in the day-to-day life of the city—and in the day-to-day lives of black children.

Our reaction to this teacher's response to Martin's presentation does not imply that we believe that the students' *being black* should have been the *only* consideration in the teacher's interaction with her black students. More broadly, Martin argued for teachers of mathematics to move beyond demographic data and reflect on those identities that might be most salient and important to students and to understand how these identities might shape student and teacher engagement with school mathematics. Although Martin's experiences focused on black children, all students bring both school and life experiences to the classroom, and these have an impact not only on how they perceive themselves as mathematics learners but also on how others see them. A goal for all teachers should be to learn enough about these experiences to engage, support, and teach all students, whether they are black students from an urban context, new immigrant students in a rural town, or affluent students in a private school.

Throughout this book, we argue that a number of identity-related issues can emerge as being relevant to how teachers support mathematics learning of their students in different contexts. How teachers recognize and respond to these issues will have an impact on how they address the questions raised at the beginning of this chapter.

Rethinking Equity

Although the focus of this book is on helping teachers develop equity-oriented practices in relation to mathematics, we embrace a perspective on equity that supports teaching practices and reflective tools focused on empowerment of the whole child. As a result, this equity-based approach includes attending to the multiple identities—racial, ethnic, cultural, linguistic, gender, mathematical, and so on—that students develop and draw on as they learn and do mathematics. In support of this holistic view of equity, we offer the following description of what we believe teachers owe to all students:

All students, in light of their humanity—their personal experiences, backgrounds, histories, languages, and physical and emotional well-being—must have the opportunity and support to learn rich mathematics that fosters meaning making, empowers decision making, and critiques, challenges, and transforms inequities and injustices. Equity does not mean that every student should receive identical instruction. Instead, equity demands that responsive accommodations be made as needed to promote equitable access, attainment, and advancement in mathematics education for each student.

This perspective on equity challenges common notions that students need to learn math "in spite of" or "regardless of" who they are. We argue that students need to learn mathematics *in light of* who they are and the diverse gifts that they bring to their experiences every day. In the case of Danny Martin and the young teacher, this more holistic view of equity-based teaching practice would require attending to and understanding black children's emerging and developing racial identities in the context of local and larger social realities in which they live every day. In the case of Baye, it would mean understanding how all the different experiences in Baye's school life, home life, faith life, athletic life, and cultural life may affect the ways that he experiences school mathematics and that he, his father, and his teacher see him as a mathematics learner. Furthermore, this equity perspective demands attention to the ways that societal views of mathematics performance may fuel stereotypes (for example, the notion that Asian students are good at math) and obstruct the development of a positive mathematics identity.

We also recognize that this holistic view means embracing life complexities that may support and *challenge* children to learn mathematics and develop their mathematics identities. Teachers can inspire students beyond or apart from difficult life circumstances, and they can take advantage of strengths that all children bring to school. They also can disrupt or eliminate, rather than perpetuate, negative images of what it means to learn mathematics and beliefs about who can learn mathematics. They can develop strong partnerships with parents to support a child's learning of mathematics.

Conclusion

This book offers guidance and support to rethink instructional practice and embrace an equity orientation to promote positive mathematics learning and identity development. Enriching one's practice in this way takes conviction and courage. Reflecting on these possibilities and their impact on instructional practices is key. However, taking *action* to change instructional practice in ways that can strengthen student learning and cultivate a positive mathematics identity, particularly in children who continue to be marginalized, is the most critical step in empowering young people mathematically.

DISCUSSION QUESTIONS

1. Why is mathematics important for students to learn? Whose interests are served by the reasons that you give?

2. If you could consult with Ms. Carlson and Baye's father, what would you discuss about how best to support Baye as a math learner? Reflect on why those discussion points are important in relation to mathematics learning and identity.

3. Reflect on Danny Martin's viewpoint that it is important for teachers of mathematics to consider the interaction of racial identity and mathematics identity in children's experiences of learning school mathematics. Do you have questions about this perspective?

DISCUSSION QUESTIONS—*CONTINUED*

4. After reading this chapter and reflecting on the examples in it, what questions do you have about the impact of a student's math identity on his or her mathematics confidence and competence? What strategies have you used to learn about the school and life experiences of students in your classroom?

5. How does your own perspective on equity connect with the equity issues discussed in this chapter?

Chapter 2

Identities, Agency, and Mathematical Proficiency: What Teachers Need to Know to Support Student Learning

Consider the comments of Terrell, a fourteen-year-old boy, about himself:

> Ever since I started playing hockey, my dad has been on my case to do my work. Keep my grades up in school. If I don't, that's the end of my hockey career. The most respect I get is from hockey.... I want to be the best in hockey, so I work hard in school to be able to play hockey.... People think of hockey as a white man's sport. But I think if a man wants to play hockey or a man wants to do something he wants to do, then he should be able to do it without anybody questioning how he does it or why he does it.

Terrell was one of thirty-five students interviewed as part of a larger research study that focused on academic and mathematics success and failure among African American middle school students (Martin 2000). Analysis of this excerpt, and the longer interview from which it came, showed that Terrell's strong identity as a hockey player served to strengthen his identity as a good mathematics student and helped to keep him among the highest achievers in his school.

A central goal of this chapter is to discuss the inextricable links between mathematics learning and identity. Specifically, we focus on some of the many forces that shape students' *mathematics identities*—how students see themselves and how they are seen by others, including teachers, parents, and peers, as doers of mathematics. We also give attention to other identities that students develop in and out of school and discuss how those identities shape and are shaped by students' life experiences. Then we discuss the concepts of *mathematical agency* and *mathematical proficiency* to highlight important behaviors, dispositions, and skills that teachers can help students strengthen to support positive mathematics identities. We conclude the chapter with a discussion of how teachers can reframe the identities that they ascribe to students—identities that might be based on stereotypes or limited knowledge of student backgrounds—to help strengthen mathematics teaching and learning in the classroom.

What Is Identity, and Why Should Teachers Be Concerned about It?

Identities can be defined as "the ways that people come to conceptualize themselves and others" and how they act as a result of those understandings (Cornell and Hartmann 1998, p. xvii). Identities can emerge in the form of *stories* that announce to the world who we think we are, who we want to become, or who we are not.

Student identities are diverse and complex. They can be faith-based—strong Muslim or Christian identities, perhaps—and family-based—identities as "good sons" or "good daughters," for instance. Identities of young people can also include early identifications with careers as doctors, lawyers, teachers, engineers, or sports professionals, for example. These identities are important; they can serve as sources of strength and motivation to do well in school, in general, and in mathematics, in particular (Martin 2000).

We believe that children's developing identities should be important considerations in the daily work of all teachers. Teaching involves not only developing important skills and conceptual understanding in mathematics but also supporting students' coming to see themselves as legitimate and powerful doers of mathematics. This understanding of children's identities, especially in relation to mathematics, can give teachers a better understanding of how and why some students make positive connections with mathematics and others do not. With this enhanced understanding, teachers can adjust their practice to support and strengthen a child's learning of mathematics and his or her persistence as a confident mathematical learner.

What Are Mathematics Identities?

We define *mathematics identity* as the dispositions and deeply held beliefs that students develop about their ability to participate and perform effectively in mathematical contexts and to use mathematics in powerful ways across the contexts of their lives. Depending on the context, a mathematics identity may reflect a sense of oneself as a competent performer who is able to do mathematics or as the kind of person who is unable to do mathematics.

Mathematics identities can be expressed in story form. These stories reflect not only what we say and believe about ourselves as mathematics learners but also how others see us in relation to mathematics. Teachers, peers, and parents can all exert an influence on the mathematics identities that students develop. A key consideration about mathematics identities is that they are strongly connected with the other identities that students construct and view as important in their lives, including their racial, gender, language, cultural, ethnic, family, faith, and academic identities.

For example, Berry (2008) interviewed and observed six African American middle school boys who were able to reflect on their mathematical experiences and how those experiences shaped their mathematics identities. Although Berry was interested in how these boys learned and saw themselves in relation to *mathematics*, he did not minimize attention to their *racial* identities as African Americans, because both of these identities were salient in the school experiences of these boys. One of those interviewed was Cordell, whose narrative provides a glimpse of his emerging mathematics, academic, "good son," and African American identities and shows how his experiences in and out of school wove those identities together.

My name is Cordell, and I am an eighth-grade student at Memorial Middle School. I am an only child, and I live with my mother. I know that my mother, being a single parent, has a tough job, so I have had to take on more responsibilities than other kids do, and I have learned to be independent. My grandmother and aunts help my mother by encouraging me to make good decisions and make sure that I stay on the right track. My grandmother and mother talk to me about doing well in school and make sure I do my work. My mother is always saying I better do well in school if I plan on going to college.

Math is my favorite subject because it is my easiest subject. Math is interesting and fun because in math you have to think and keep trying until you get it right. I was first drawn to math in the third grade when we started to learn how to multiply. I knew I was good because I learned to multiply earlier than the other kids in my class. I am glad that I was good at math at a young age, because that put me ahead of the other kids in my class. My third-grade teacher divided the class into groups, and I was with the group that got the harder problems. This made me feel like I was smart.

When I was in fourth grade, I started getting into trouble because I was bored with school. My teacher was teaching me things I already knew, so I would start playing around in class. My mother thought I was not being challenged enough and that is why I got into trouble. After a few conferences with the teacher and the principal, my mother felt that I should be tested for the AG [academically gifted] program. The teacher and principal did not want me tested because they felt I was not gifted. My mother thinks the reason they did not want to test me was because I am Black. She stayed on the teachers and principals until I was tested. I did well enough to be placed in the AG program midway through my fourth-grade year.

Cordell's narrative reveals a number of identities that are important to him and that are interwoven in his sense of self as a mathematics student. These identities include being a middle school student, an only child, an independent good son, a self-acknowledged smart student, and a black boy who some school officials think is not gifted in mathematics. Cordell's narrative also helps to demonstrate our claim that students negotiate a number of complex identities that emerge as important to them. These identities can find support in parents and teachers and other significant people in students' lives.

As Cordell's narrative helps to demonstrate, both parents and teachers can have profound influences on their children's mathematics identities in response to the messages that they send about their competencies and abilities. These messages can emerge in the stories that children tell about their mathematical experiences.

It is important to note that mathematics identities emerge not only through the stories that students tell and that are told about them but also through the *behaviors* that they demonstrate to help position themselves as certain kinds of people (for example, good math students) or as members of a particular group (high achievers, for instance). A student's correct and confident use of mathematical language and argumentation strategies, supported by positive feedback from teachers and peers, could help to reflect or shape a positive mathematical identity. These identity-affirming (or identity-challenging) behaviors can influence the kinds of learning experiences and social relations that students have with others (Cornell and Hartman 1998). A student who has been identified and behaves as a "gifted" mathematics student among her peers may dominate classroom interactions and activities in an attempt to maintain her status. A student who believes that he is not good at mathematics may remain silent in small-group interactions because he fears that other students will judge him. Language-intensive practices that demand increased levels of math discourse may come to favor or privilege some students (native English speakers, students who are outspoken) over others (English language learners, shy students), allowing the former to assume leadership roles, elevate their status as doers of mathematics, and improve their mathematics communication skills.

Similarly, classroom activities that reward speed as ideal mathematics behavior may lead students to believe that being "good at mathematics" means being able to recite multiplication facts or carry out calculations quickly. Students who are more deliberate in their work may see themselves as being not good at mathematics. Moreover, as criteria emerge to establish who gets labeled as "smart" or "gifted" or "slow" or "proficient" or "at-risk," students will come to see themselves in particular ways relative to other members of their mathematical communities. Instead of becoming more valued members of their classroom communities, they may come to see themselves as outsiders.

Thus, many influences shape a student's mathematical identity—some negative and some positive. It is important for teachers to understand the impact of the instructional decisions that they make, and the social and academic norms that they create, on a child's mathematics identity.

Mathematical agency

The definition of mathematics identity presented earlier in this chapter includes "the ability to participate and perform effectively in mathematical contexts." This behavioral aspect of mathematics identity can also be captured by the term *agency*. Several mathematics educators have taken up the idea of *mathematical agency* and documented it among students and teachers in classroom settings. Turner (2003), for example, has drawn on her work with Mexican American and Mexican children in the Southwestern United States to conceptualize *critical mathematical agency* as students' capacity to "identify themselves as powerful mathematical thinkers who construct rigorous mathematical understandings, and who participate in mathematics in personally and socially meaningful ways" (p. iv). Gresalfi and colleagues (2009) characterized agency in terms of opportunities to complete mathematical tasks, and they distinguished two forms of mathematical agency: *disciplinary agency* and *conceptual agency*:

Recalling facts or definitions and executing procedures involve disciplinary agency; there are correct answers, and a student either gets it right or doesn't. Procedures with connections and, especially, doing mathematics generally involve conceptual agency, with students being positioned to take initiative in constructing meaning and understanding of the methods and concepts that are the subjects of their learning. (p. 56)

Both Turner's and Gresalfi and colleagues' conceptualizations of agency help to highlight that students are active participants in, rather than passive recipients of, their mathematics education experiences. They can exercise these forms of agency in productive ways—resisting negative identities that are imposed on them, developing mathematical strategies within the context of small-group work, or using mathematics as a tool to understand their life circumstances or events in the world. Creating opportunities for students—particularly those who traditionally have had less access to powerful mathematics and mathematical practices—to engage in productive forms of agency should be a goal for all teachers.

The idea of mathematical agency is not confined to individual students. Classrooms of students can exhibit *collective mathematical agency* when teachers and their students act together to solve problems, working from the shared belief that viable strategies can be developed and solutions can be found. Different students can contribute different elements to this collective agency. Some students might contribute productive reasoning strategies. Other students might make computational contributions. Others might contribute through whole-class explanations of particular mathematical concepts or by asking questions that help to clarify problems and concepts for themselves and their classmates. Teachers can also encourage students to assume various roles that provide them with opportunities to make viable contributions to classroom activities and practices. Some students with bilingual competencies might be assigned roles as translators for their peers whose first language is not English, so that these students will not be left behind. Teachers can further contribute to this collective agency by helping to establish classroom norms and rules for behavior that encourage cooperation and risk taking during problem solving rather than strict competition (Featherstone et al. 2011; Horn 2012).

Reflective teacher practice that is committed to equity will include the development of tasks, activities, and classroom cultures that encourage students to exercise their positive mathematical agency, individually and collectively. These forms of agency can contribute to students' developing positive identity-related stories and behaviors that affirm and demonstrate these identities.

Mathematical proficiency

Creating these expanded opportunities for students to learn mathematics and develop productive mathematics identities with powerful agency will also require teachers to develop a broader concept of what counts as mathematics proficiency. As outlined in *Adding It Up: Helping Children Learn Mathematics* (National Research Council 2001a), teaching for mathematical proficiency no longer should include a singular focus on having students develop computation skills and memorize algorithms, perhaps privileging those students who believe mathematics is about doing computations quickly. As the book suggests (see fig. 2.1), mathematical proficiency should include developing *conceptual understanding* (comprehension of mathematical concepts, operations, and relations), *procedural fluency* (skill in carrying out procedures flexibly, accurately, efficiently, and appropriately), *strategic competence* (the ability to formulate, represent, and solve mathematical problems), *adaptive reasoning* (the capacity for logical thought, reflection, explanation, and justification), and *productive disposition* (a habitual inclination to see mathematics as sensible, useful, and worthwhile, coupled with a belief in diligence and one's own efficacy).

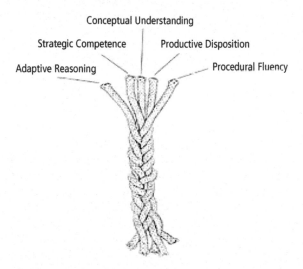

Conceptual Understanding

Strategic Competence   Productive Disposition

Adaptive Reasoning   Procedural Fluency

Fig. 2.1. Five strands of mathematical proficiency
(National Research Council 2001a, p. 5; reprinted by permission)

Although the five strands of mathematical proficiency outlined in *Adding It Up* are intertwined, as the figure suggests, one or more may emerge earlier in some students than in others. Some students might demonstrate deep conceptual understanding but might not yet demonstrate strong strategic competence. Other students might demonstrate strong procedural fluency but might not yet display a productive disposition toward certain kinds of tasks and practices. Teachers will need to reflect on which classroom and curricular practices provide the best opportunities for these components of mathematical proficiency to emerge.

These expanded themes related to mathematics proficiency can also be found in the mathematical practices identified and emphasized in the Common Core State Standards for Mathematics (National Governors Association Center for Best Practices and Council of Chief State School Officers 2010). The Standards for Mathematical Practice "describe ways in which developing student practitioners of the discipline of mathematics increasingly ought to engage with the subject matter as they grow in mathematical maturity and expertise" (p. 8):

1. Make sense of problems and persevere in solving them.

2. Reason abstractly and quantitatively.

3. Construct viable arguments and critique the reasoning of others.

4. Model with mathematics.

5. Use appropriate tools strategically.

6. Attend to precision.

7. Look for and make use of structure.

8. Look for and express regularity in repeated reasoning.

We believe that these shifts in characterizing mathematical proficiency can help to foster reflective and equitable mathematics practice among teachers *and* the development of positive identifications with mathematics among students. Instructionally, these shifts offer teachers an increased number of pathways and points of entry to assess students' mathematical development. For students, these broader conceptions of mathematical proficiency provide multiple ways to demonstrate their competence. That is, these expanded possibilities for developing and demonstrating mathematics competence can represent substantial opportunities to learn and engage in mathematics. We believe that *how* students experience mathematics in their classrooms shapes their views of mathematics and themselves as mathematics learners and doers. Thus, how mathematical proficiency is defined and communicated to students has a powerful impact on their mathematics identities and their exercise of various forms of agency.

Seeing the Multiple Identities of Students

Although we give primacy to mathematics, we emphasize the importance of recognizing the range of identities beyond mathematics that students spend their time and energy developing or that others may assign to them. Acknowledging these identities can lead to richer, more meaningful understanding of children and their lives. Terrell's identities as a hockey player and a good student, for example, serve to challenge popular societal and school-based perceptions and negative stereotypes about what it means to be a young African American male. It is important to note that although Terrell was able to defy negative stereotypes by maintaining high grades in mathematics, expressing positive attitudes toward mathematics, and demonstrating classroom behaviors typically associated with being a good mathematics student, he did not identify mathematics as his favorite subject or use mathematics as the *primary* source for constructing his overall academic identity. In fact, English was Terrell's favorite school subject:

I like English because I like to write. I'm not much of a poem writer but I want to write poems. That's what I want to do. Nobody knows. I never told anybody that I want to write poems, but that's what I want to do. So, I like English. My mentor is Langston Hughes. I look up to him.

These remarks by Terrell serves to remind us that, unless asked, students may be unwilling to reveal important aspects of their many developing identities. Similarly, students can be very adept at invoking particular identities to serve particular needs in both school and nonschool contexts.

It is equally important to stress the significance of identity-based considerations for students whose identities are often taken for granted. In many school-based discussions and policies, the categories "Asian" and "Latina/o or Hispanic," for example, are often associated with beliefs about students who do well in school, in the case of the former category, and with children who struggle and fail, in the case of the latter category. Often these associations exist with no consideration of the varied experiences of different subgroups and the varied home and cultural experiences and roles of children within those subgroups.

Orellana (2009) highlights the family roles of immigrant children and the complex identities they take on in relation to both their family and school lives. She offers a brief profile of a fourteen-year-old girl, Cindy, and describes her role as family translator. Orellana explains that Cindy liked this role because "she learned more about other people in her family and about herself…; it made her feel smart; she learned more words in her two languages, English and Chinese" (p. 9). In describing how she believed these experiences distinguished her from her peers, Cindy was simultaneously able to reveal the out-of-school mathematical needs (for example, budgeting and making banking transactions) that she was meeting to ensure her family's well-being:

Sometimes I think I invaded people's privacy, like they have to tell me over the phone, like deposit statements and stuff like that. I know exactly the house's wages and stuff like that, and I tell my parents, and they don't really care. I just know, and I translate it. While the other kids, they ask for things, I'm not trodding down people of my own age, but some people they just ask for things, like "Can I have a bike, can I go swimming, can I go to summer camp, can I have a new pair of Nikes?"… Their parents keep saying, "Do you know how hard I work for the money to pay bills?" They don't know exactly how much is in their bank deposits, the bills and stuff. But *I* know personally because I write the bills. I write the checks. (Orellana 2009, p. 9)

In Cindy's case, her family roles and out-of-school experiences helped to shape her identity as a daughter, a translator, and a budget manager. Her identities intersect with one another in ways that reveal complexities that nonimmigrant children may not experience.

Our point in presenting the preceding examples is to stress that *all* students develop, resist, and try on many different identities as they make sense of their experiences in school and nonschool contexts. These identities, in our view, are important in shaping how students come to see themselves as mathematics learners.

Reframing Identities to Strengthen Mathematics Learning

We encourage teachers to take an active role in shaping positive mathematics identities among their students by also attending to the other identities that students are developing. But to succeed, teachers must do so in ways that move away from negative stereotypes (such as identifying black males as thugs or identifying Latina/o and Asian children as "illegal aliens" or "anchor babies") and avoid reducing children to nameless, objectified data points (as "bubble kids," for instance) in larger conversations about assessment. Increased awareness and understanding of students' multiple and complex identities may require that teachers move beyond the simple categories that seem to work for sorting and ranking purposes. Demographic and socioeconomic labels such as "black," "white," "Latina/o or Hispanic," "Asian," "Native American," "immigrant," "urban," "rural," "middle-class," "gifted," "limited English proficient," "bilingual," "at-risk," "disabled," and "poor" are common in school discourse but are often used in ways that mask their complexity and intersection.

We ask teachers to reflect on how their students might make sense of these labels and categories. Understanding how and why students come to resist or accept particular labels can be helpful in understanding their engagement or lack of engagement in mathematics. For example, do students internalize positive or negative stereotypes about mathematical intelligence and ability that are associated with their own or others' racial and ethnic identities? In the context of discussions of racial achievement gaps, do students who identify themselves as "Native American" or "African American" or "Latina/o" see themselves as intellectually inferior to students who are identified as "white" or "Asian"? What effects do discussions about "illegal" immigration have on the academic engagement of undocumented students or students with undocumented family members? How do students from various Asian subgroups respond to stereotypes about mathematical superiority or the expectations that come with being labeled as a "model minority"?

As teachers reflect on how they might simultaneously support and affirm students' racial, gender, cultural, ethnic, academic, and mathematics identities, we encourage them to seek ways to reframe negative views of the identities that reflect limited knowledge of students' background experiences and social realities. We offer some examples and suggestions in the discussion that follows.

From acceptance of, to resistance to, "model minority" myths

Societal and educational discourse often holds up students who are identified as "Asian," "Southeast Asian," and "East Indian" as "model minorities" in comparison with students who are identified as "African American," "Latina/o," or "Native American." Such discourse communicates the idea that Asian students are academically superior, come from cultures and families that value education, and have successfully assimilated into American society. Because Asian American students have minority status and are perceived as having overcome language and cultural barriers to achieve their success, the belief is widespread that students from other minority groups should be able to overcome their circumstances and achieve at much higher levels. Instead of assuming that African American, Latina/o, and Native American students come from racial and cultural backgrounds where education is valued, the dominant narratives suggest that "cultural deficits" are the cause of underachievement by these children.

Several Asian American scholars, including Lee (2005, 2009) and Louie (2004), for example, have challenged the idea of the Asian model minority and have pointed out that this characterization of schooling experiences often overlooks the educational struggles of various Asian American subgroups, including Laotian, Hmong, Mien, and Cambodian students. This myth also overlooks the experiences of poor and working-class Chinese and Vietnamese students, for example, who may not be high achievers but may drop out of school or be on the verge of doing so. As a result of the myth, these students are not likely to receive the support services that they need to improve their academic standing or help them remain in school.

We suggest that teachers reflect critically on this myth and understand that Asian American students are varied and diverse in their identities and backgrounds. Furthermore, their mathematics experiences, like their experiences in broader societal contexts, reflect the impact of issues of race, class, gender, and culture.

From limited English to multilingual language brokers

Many states and cities are experiencing changes in demographics that often bring dozens of languages into their schools and classrooms. When children from culturally and linguistically diverse backgrounds enter school, their home language and language status often become primary markers for their identities. How teachers respond to these language identities is important. We know, for example, that these students are typically referred to as "limited English proficient," with "limited" as the operative word. Although this assignment of identity to these children is accurate to a certain degree, it is itself limited. These students are in the process of becoming bilingual or multilingual, with English becoming for them a second, or even a third, language.

The label "limited English" masks the multilingual backgrounds and experiences of many students. The reality is that many of these children are positioned within their families as *language brokers* who must navigate nonschool contexts on behalf of their parents, despite their age and evolving development as English speakers. As we noted earlier in the case of Cindy's story, researchers have documented these brokering practices among students and families who have immigrated from Mexico, Central America, China, Hong Kong, and Korea. Orellana (2009) offers useful descriptions of these children's roles as language brokers:

> Children serve as language brokers because their families need their skills in order to accomplish the tasks of everyday life in their new linguistic and cultural context. Many teachers also need these children's skills. (p. 2)

> Language brokering involves activities in which children, often taking the lead with adults, facilitate their parents' abilities to accomplish what these adults would not be able to accomplish on their own. In the process, children also support their parents' acquisition of English language and literacy skills. (p. 104)

Bilingual children also serve as language brokers in the classroom by performing bilingual translations and mediations of oral and written texts from their first language to English and vice versa. They act in this role for their peers as well as their teachers (Manyak 2004). In addition, recent research has demonstrated the connection of language-brokering practices with increased levels of academic performance (Dorner, Orellana, and Li-Grining 2007).

In the case of mathematics classrooms, we would argue that bilingual students at various levels of English proficiency can spontaneously find themselves serving as, or being positioned by others to serve as, language brokers during classroom interactions. More important, these students can bring to mathematics learning considerable strengths that may go unrecognized if the instructional focus is only on the use of English vocabulary and pronunciation rather than on additional ways in which these students are communicating their ideas through gestures, representations, and their first languages.

For example, Moschkovich (2002) highlighted the ways in which Latina/o bilingual students used an array of resources that supported their own and their peers' learning. During a middle school math class, students constructed rectangles of the same area (36 square units) and different perimeters while looking for patterns that related the perimeter to the dimensions of the rectangles. During a small-group discussion, one group of Latina girls spoke primarily in Spanish while attempting to solve the problem. They struggled to come up with the Spanish word for "rectangle," using other words, such as *ángulo* ("angle"), *triángulo* ("triangle"), and *rángulo* ("rangle") in their problem-solving efforts. Later, the teacher asked the small groups to present their ideas about mathematical relationships between the perimeter and the dimensions of the rectangle, and one of the students in the small group, Alicia, responded:

The longer the, ah… the longer [traces the shape of a long rectangle with her hands several times] the, ah… the longer the rángulo [rangle], you know the more the perimeter, the higher the perimeter is. (p. 201)

What is important to note is that as the group's spokesperson, Alicia was serving in a role as a language broker for her group, for her peers, and for her teacher. She communicated a mathematical idea in English that was developed in her small group discussions that occurred primarily in Spanish. Although she did not use the correct term, *rectangle*, in the explanation, the way in which she used gestures and mathematical objects such as drawings of rectangles conveyed the group's collective understanding of a relationship between the shape of the rectangle (with longer lengths) and the perimeter. Moschkovich (2002) notes the completeness of the explanation: "Although Alicia was missing crucial vocabulary, she did appropriately (in the right place, at the right time, and in the right way) use a construction commonly used in mathematical communities to describe patterns, make comparisons, and describe direct variation: "The longer the ____, the more (higher) the____" (p. 203).

Focusing only on the limited use of correct English vocabulary and pronunciation rather than on the mathematical ideas and language that Alicia did communicate could negatively affect Alicia's and her group's views of their mathematical competence. Shifting to a language-broker perspective enhances teachers' opportunities to recognize the multiple resources and responsibilities that bilingual learners bring to mathematics learning and participation.

From "at-risk" to "resilient"

Quite often, the discourse about students who come from backgrounds that are not middle-class or wealthy is characterized by negative assumptions about their skills, abilities, competencies, and motivation. For example, if students are identified as "poor," assumptions attaching to this label might include the belief that little teaching or learning occurs in their homes and communities. In our experiences in school contexts and discussions with colleagues, we have frequently encountered opinions like the following: "These children come from bad neighborhoods. Their parents don't care. They don't value education. They have too many hurdles in their lives to focus on learning. These children can't learn algebra." These attitudes represent very limited conceptions of children, their families, and their competencies.

Even if students come from backgrounds characterized by poverty and limited resources, they often exhibit high levels of resilience and mathematical excellence in the face of these circumstances (Martin 2000). For example, Turner and Celedón-Pattichis (2011) analyzed the problem-solving competencies of Latina/o bilingual kindergartners. These students exhibited mathematical excellence in solving increasingly complex word problems and showcased various strategies for correctly solving problems involving multiplication and division. These children from working-class immigrant families in the Southwest demonstrated mathematical success equal to that of wealthier students, according to assessments from an earlier study.

Studies like these continue to challenge commonly held deficit views of children from poor and working-class backgrounds, students of color, and English learners as automatically "at risk" by virtue of their racial, ethnic, and socioeconomic backgrounds and levels of English proficiency. We argue that a focus on learning rather than on labeling is critical. Furthermore, finding ways to build on this resilience, rather than focus solely on the conditions that make such resilience necessary, should be primary goals for teachers.

Conclusion

In this chapter, we have encouraged teachers to engage in deeper reflection not only on the mathematics that they will teach but also on the multiple identities that emerge as important to their students and how those identities can shape, and be shaped by, mathematics learning and classroom engagement. We claim that if teachers are to support the development of positive mathematics identities and multiple forms of mathematical proficiency and mathematical agency, they must also develop a deeper understanding of these multiple identities and the social realities of their students. We encourage teachers to understand the productive identities that students are developing and to reframe the negative identities in ways that move beyond stereotypes and simplicity.

DISCUSSION QUESTIONS

1. What range of mathematics identities are expressed and performed by your students? What actions do you take to positively affirm your students' mathematics identities? What are some ways that you might get students to share their emerging mathematics identities?

2. What are some of the various identities that your students express and perform through the stories that they narrate in your mathematics classroom? In what ways do these identities support or hinder the development of positive mathematics identities?

DISCUSSION QUESTIONS—*CONTINUED*

3. What are some of the ways that students demonstrate their mathematical agency in your classroom? How do you model positive mathematical agency and provide opportunities for students to demonstrate this?

4. What are some of the stereotypes and assumptions that emerge in your classroom about who can or cannot do mathematics? How do you and your students deal with these stereotypes and assumptions?

5. What additional family roles do your students take on that might contribute to their positive development in mathematics?

Chapter 3

Know Thyself: What Shapes Mathematics Teacher Identities?

In chapter 2, we defined *identity* as the stories that people tell about themselves and what they view as important to them: their understanding of their place in the world and their core beliefs. We can also perform an identity as one way to let others know the kind of person we claim to be. These stories and performances are multifaceted, dynamic, and grow out of our experiences in multiple contexts—school, home, sports, family traditions, media, careers, and so forth. Our identities represent negotiations between who we claim to be and how others identify and label us. Teachers' professional identities—which can be thought of as their "sense of self as well as their knowledge, beliefs, interests, dispositions, and orientations toward their work and change" (Drake, Spillane, and Hufford-Ackles 2001, p. 2)—are also negotiated and shaped across experiences in a number of contexts, including university credential programs, professional development, district policies, school relationships, and professional learning communities (Beijaard, Meijer, and Verloop 2004; Olsen 2011).

The purpose of this chapter is to examine experiences and contexts that can contribute to the development of a K–8 *mathematics teacher identity*—an identity that consists of knowledge and lived experiences, interweaving to inform teaching views, dispositions, and practices to help children learn mathematics (Drake, Spillane, and Hufford-Ackles 2001; Gresalfi and Cobb 2011). In focusing on mathematics teacher identity, we acknowledge that it is just one of many disciplinary identities that K–8 teachers develop and that it can inform and shape their teaching practice. For example, some elementary teachers might be avid readers and passionate about helping students learn to read. This might lead them to integrate literacy strategies across different subjects to deepen students' skills and passion for reading. A middle school teacher who was formerly a wildlife biologist and who loves science might have chosen teaching as a second career to share her enthusiasm for science with young people. Another teacher might also be an artist, motivating him to find different ways to infuse art across the curriculum. In all these cases, a specific disciplinary passion can shape a teacher's professional identity and instructional practice.

This chapter discusses a range of personal and professional experiences that can contribute to the development of a mathematics teacher identity. We start with teachers' stories of their own mathematics learning experiences. These stories are math autobiographies of new teachers just entering the profession. The stories represent a wide array of experiences with mathematics in and out of school, including specific challenges and supports that shaped the teachers' mathematics learning, as well as ways that these experiences shaped their teaching vision for mathematics learning in their own classrooms. Furthermore, we discuss how those experiences were shaped, in turn, by race, class, gender, and language. By drawing on personal narratives from new teachers, we focus additional attention on elements that influence the development of mathematics teacher identity in its early stages and are perhaps somewhat disconnected from current views of mathematics teacher identity.

We also explore the unique role that the high status of mathematics as a subject in the K–8 curriculum plays in how teachers see themselves in relation to their work and their students. In many schools, mathematics is a centerpiece of a school improvement plan. In the face of calls to increase access to and the rigor of school mathematics experienced by students in our schools (for example, the Common Core State Standards for Mathematics and eighth-grade algebra mandates), these demands can lead some teachers to question how effective they can be in helping their students learn mathematics. Teachers may also develop beliefs that conflict with demands about what math topics should be taught to which students. Thus, a teacher's acceptance or rejection of such changes exposes important elements of his or her mathematics teacher identity. The chapter concludes with a series of discussion questions aimed to motivate reflection on mathematics teacher identity and how it shapes your practice in the classroom.

Teachers as Math Learners

The nature of the mathematics learning experiences that a teacher had in his or her own schooling has a powerful influence on the mathematics teacher identity that he or she develops (Drake, Spillane, and Hufferd-Ackles 2001). Because a mathematics teacher identity is, at least partly, rooted in a teacher's experiences as a mathematics learner, we must explore how those experiences may have been shaped, in turn, by race, class, gender, and language. Below, we discuss these interconnections by examining the mathematics autobiographies of six new teachers (all of whose names have been changed). Taken together, these stories help to provide an understanding of how teachers' identities as mathematics learners shape their mathematics teacher identities and how these mathematics teacher identities, in turn, influence the decisions and actions enacted in K–8 mathematics classrooms.

Shawna Jamison: Middle school mathematics intervention teacher

Shawna is a new middle school mathematics teacher with a K–8 multiple subjects teaching credential and a special education endorsement. Her attitude toward math has evolved over time. Shawna grew up in a white, middle-class family. Until high school, her school peers came from similar racial and class backgrounds. Although her high school was more racially diverse, her peers in advanced mathematics courses tended to be primarily middle class and white, with some Asian American students. At home, her parents provided "many math learning opportunities," including baking (measuring ingredients, for instance), gardening (planting seeds in relation to sunlight and area or volume of soil), and softball (batting averages, earned-run averages, and so forth). In elementary school, Shawna loved to explore math concepts in class. She thrived on solving math problems on worksheets; math seemed "easy and enjoyable." During her teenage years, mathematics became less important. Although she pursued mathematics through high school calculus, she claimed that she "did not take responsibility" for her learning. When she attended the large public university in her state, her performance on the math placement test resulted in her having to retake precalculus. This placement led to a difficult time in her mathematics learning experience. The university precalculus class was huge, and she found herself unmotivated to attend class or seek help. She decided to withdraw from the class and change her major to psychology, which required very little math. Shawna successfully graduated with her bachelor's degree. She returned to school eight years later to pursue a course of study leading to a teaching career. However, she needed a mathematics class to enter the teaching credential program. She decided to retake precalculus at the local community college. With the help of a supportive and knowledgeable professor, peer collaboration, and her own perseverance, she rediscovered her fondness for mathematics.

> The class work was challenging, but accessible. I was motivated and engaged. Before tests, I studied with other students in the class. While it was difficult to take the risk of being an engaged math student after all these years and math failures, the sense of pride I felt in my math achievement was priceless.

Shawna's evolved attitude toward mathematics and her own mathematics learning shaped her commitment to teaching mathematics at the middle school level, particularly to students who might struggle with mathematics:

> Watching the students struggle reminds me of myself as I struggled with math. I can relate to not wanting to try for fear of failure. While I grew up in a very different environment than most of these students, the same things that helped me get back on track with math will help them; feeling like a valuable contributor to a community of learners, curriculum that is challenging and appropriate for their level, and motivation to learn.

Clearly, Shawna empathized with mathematically struggling students because of her own experience as a math learner. She also perceived "environment" differences between her own childhood experience and those of most of the students she worked with in the math intervention courses.

Shawna's math schooling experiences were characterized by a lack of interaction with racially and ethnically diverse peers. However, her first assignment was teaching math intervention courses in a school that served large populations of black, Latino/a, and Vietnamese students. In addition, many of her students "lived in poverty." She viewed the similarities and differences between herself and her middle school students in a positive light. Although some teachers might have found these middle school students frustrating, given their academic and socioeconomic backgrounds, Shawna viewed working in the mathematics intervention courses as "an exciting opportunity to empower these students." She believed that what had worked for her in overcoming her mathematics struggles—encouragement to make valuable contributions, "challenging and appropriate" curriculum, and motivation to learn—could also work for her students. This positive attitude framed her vision and beliefs about what makes an effective mathematics teacher and helped to shape her instructional practice in her classroom.

Leslie Park: Third-grade elementary teacher

Leslie is a new third-grade teacher with a general K–8 multiple subjects teaching credential. Growing up, Leslie had negative feelings about mathematics because she associated it with academic intelligence. However she found comfort in the fact that she believed mathematics always had a "right answer" and that memorizing formulas and following procedures was how to excel in mathematics. Leslie identified herself as Asian American. She grew up in a small rural town with a large agricultural industry. Leslie attended school with primarily white, middle-class or wealthy peers. She described herself as an "oddball," not only because she was a member of a racial minority in her school (one of two Asian American students in the school), but also because she struggled with the model minority myth and stereotypes related to being Asian and excelling in mathematics.

> The truth is, I didn't just want to be good in math, I wanted to excel. This is because I associated intelligence with the ability to do math. Perhaps this is something that the society has ingrained in me but it was what I believed. And because I wasn't good in math, I felt like I was not smart. There is a stereotype of Asians being math geniuses. Being an Asian American myself, I sometimes felt embarrassed because I did not fit into the Asian mold.

In high school, Leslie had ups and downs in her mathematics success. She did quite well in ninth-grade algebra but proceeded to get a C in tenth-grade geometry. She remarked, "Shapes, angles, and theorems were all too complex and analytical." She also took precalculus and calculus in high school, working very hard with a tutor every day after school to obtain a grade of B. Yet, because of her self-imposed pressure to excel, she was not satisfied with such "mediocre grades." She did not fare much better in college mathematics. She started with the university's basic mathematics course involving algebra and some precalculus and "struggled through it to receive a 2.9." At that point, she decided to select a major that would "steer [her] far away from anything that involved numbers." She chose to major in English literature.

Because of her lived experiences as a struggling mathematics learner, her awareness of not conforming to the Asian American model minority myth, and her views of mathematics as procedural, with success tied to one right answer and serving as a proxy for intelligence, Leslie wanted something different for her own students.

> I do not want students to view math as a subject that is dry, formulaic, and something they have to do on their own. Rather, I want them to see it as a subject that

has many different approaches and is collaborative. In high school, I wanted so badly to be the "smart Asian girl" that I never even bothered asking my fellow classmates how they got their answer. There was no group work in math. I plan to use this personal experience that I had with math and turn it into something positive in my future classroom.

Leslie's desire to be the "smart Asian girl" in her class while struggling with mathematics demonstrates how powerful the impact of racialized and gendered experiences can be on mathematics identity. Leslie's mathematics identity deterred her from working collaboratively with her peers to learn mathematics. However, it was this math learning experience that now shaped her developing mathematics teacher identity. As an elementary teacher, she wanted to build a teaching and learning environment that was positive compared with what she experienced as a math student. She was committed to creating an environment that focused on multiple approaches to mathematics problems and leveraged collaboration.

Michael Allen: Fifth-grade elementary teacher

Michael is a fifth-grade teacher at an urban elementary school. He is a product of the school district in which he currently teaches. He grew up in a white, working-class neighborhood. He went to school with the neighborhood kids through middle school. Michael's earliest memories of mathematics included the emphasis in third grade on timed multiplication fact tests. Because he was competitive, he was disappointed about not being the fastest, yet he was also "relieved that I was not one of the slowest either." At home, he played games with his family, such as checkers, Monopoly, and various card games. Michael was interested in sports, including football and baseball, and he regularly read the sports page. Sports "brought numbers to life" for Michael:

It was vitally important to know how far out of first place [the] Cincinnati Reds or Philadelphia Phillies were. I would even calculate batting averages as soon as I realized that it was not magic or arbitrary. I credit playing football in the street with helping me learn the multiples of seven before anybody else in my third-grade class.

These mathematics experiences at home provided some support for mathematics in school. However, in sixth grade Michael had a teacher who routinely berated students for not understanding "simple procedures." For example, she claimed that there was only one way to divide fractions and that "it was easy if you know your multiplication tables." Michael worked diligently to try to find alternative ways to divide fractions:

I had to prove her wrong. I added, subtracted, multiplied, and divided my little twelve-year-old brain out. I spent time before school and after working on formulas. I even did fractions at recess, trying to figure it out. I was sure that I would solve the elusive riddle of an alternative method to dividing fractions. I came up with page-long solutions for problems [like] $3/4 \div 1/2$, all incorrect of course. I think it took me two whole days of diligent trial and error to realize that the longer I experimented, the longer and more complicated the formula became. I eventually came to the conclusion that if there was another way to solve a simple fraction division problem, it was so complicated that nobody would ever use it anyway.

Despite this situation, it was clear that Michael was comfortable with mathematics. In middle school, he found mathematics "relatively easy." However, things were different in high school. Although his high school had more racial diversity, his mathematics classes were primarily white and middle class. His mathematics grades plummeted because he refused to do homework. He characterized himself as lazy, but he always managed to "skate by" because he did well on tests. In his junior year, his mathematics teacher gave him an F. This made him academically ineligible to play football for some local private colleges, but he did manage to earn good SAT scores, which allowed him to play football at a small public institution. Unfortunately, his partying and fighting resulted in his dismissal from college. He worked for a few years and then reenrolled in community college, where he "aced" microeconomics and macroeconomics. Armed with this success, he made plans to pursue an economics degree at the large public university in his state. Economics required calculus. He started with precalculus and "bombed it." He hated the "coldness of the numbers and mathematical ideas." He switched his major to history.

Michael graduated and worked in construction for fifteen years before pursuing a teaching career. He found it "ironic" that mathematics had chased him away from economics but he used it every day in his construction management job in numerous tasks, including measuring, estimating, budgeting, and modeling. Michael's experiences with mathematics outside of school through sports, games, and construction solidified for him the importance of making mathematics relevant and linked to real-world situations and experiences. He especially wants to capitalize on the interests and natural curiosity of his students:

With my students I will try to tap into their understanding of real-world mathematics applications and their natural curiosity as a way to help them create more math knowledge and skill for themselves.

Steve Smith: New middle school science and mathematics teacher

Steve teaches seventh- and eighth-grade science, computer programming, and mathematics at an urban middle school. Steve grew up in a middle-class, white neighborhood. The demographics of his elementary, middle, and high schools were similar. Mathematics "came easy" for Steve in elementary school. His sixth-grade mathematics teacher recommended that he take the advanced seventh-grade pre-algebra mathematics class. Steve felt very honored by his teacher's confidence in his success. The seventh-grade math class proved challenging. Lacking self-confidence about being able to solve problems, Steve would try to hide behind his book. However, the teacher, in his usual way of encouraging participation and discussion in class, would regularly call on Steve to present solutions. Through hard work and persistence, and with the help of a patient teacher, Steve received an A in the course. His mathematics success continued in eighth-grade algebra, where he received one of the highest marks in the course.

However, in ninth grade, Steve transferred to a prestigious private school far away from his friends. He hit a wall in ninth-grade geometry. He could not replicate the proofs demonstrated by the teacher. He felt alienated from his classmates because he was not an athlete or a "favorite" of his teachers. He struggled through trigonometry and his first semester of precalculus. Fortunately, his precalculus teacher provided extra support, working with him after school until he understood concepts. The teacher made Steve do problems on the board and explain his thinking. According to Steve, this teacher was the first mathematics teacher who "took interest in my success and encouraged me in a positive way." Steve eventually did well in his precalculus class, and the experience encouraged him to pursue mathematics-related courses in computer programming. Later, in college, Steve decided to major in cognitive science. He excelled in the calculus, biology, and statistics courses required for the major.

Although Steve acknowledged that his mathematics experience was "largely positive," he pointed to several issues that affected his experience and image of himself as a math learner:

I have come to believe that the lack of diversity in my math education has limited my conceptual understanding and success in the field. During my geometry course, I began to assume I was not a good mathematician, because I did not learn the concepts the way they were presented to me, leading to a lower self-image. A diverse student population and an encouraging teacher could have greatly enriched my experience. Students from wholly different backgrounds than me could have brought more ideas to the table because of their life experiences.

Steve's frustration with geometry, lack of diversity in mathematics classes, and need for a patient teacher were factors in his experience that he did not want to replicate in his future mathematics teaching. On the basis of his experiences, he was determined that in his own teaching, he would encourage students to draw on different mathematical ideas and strategies to solve problems, that he would listen to and respect ideas, and that he would promote students' participation to support mathematics learning:

Encouraging all students to actively participate is necessary. If efforts are made to include all students in a class, proper respect is given to all ideas, participation is demanded and rewarded from all students, then the educational environment better will benefit all involved.

Amy Collins: New middle school science and mathematics teacher

Amy is a seventh-grade science teacher in an urban middle school. She also teaches mathematics "support" courses (math intervention classes) for students scoring below "proficient" on the annual state standardized tests. Amy attended public schools in "suburbia across America." The backgrounds of her peers were similar to her own: "Caucasian, English speaking, and middle class." Her parents were very supportive of her in school and of her interests. Her father, a former teacher, excelled in mathematics and inspired her to follow in his footsteps. Amy was identified early as a "gifted" student. This allowed her to experience two different mathematics settings in elementary school. In her "regular" classroom, mathematics was taught through a "drill and practice" approach, with students given worksheets with "hundreds of practice problems" to do at home. Amy also studied her flash cards and "aced" her tests. In her "gifted" math class, the focus was on problem solving. Students learned mathematics that was connected with their interests. For example, Amy had an early interest in architecture. She met architects and learned how to design homes, developing floor plans by calculating the area, and so on.

Amy loved mathematics and considered herself a mathematician in elementary school. However, her middle school and high school experiences in mathematics quickly challenged the positive mathematics identity that she had developed in elementary school. Amy's gendered experiences with mathematics altered her mathematics learner identity. Being a mathematician and a girl was not well accepted socially in her school.

My test scores from my other school determined my placements in my classes, which, like many at that time, were separated by ability level. I got to take algebra in middle school and relished its challenges, but I started to notice that my fellow students weren't sharing my enthusiasm for the subject, at least not the girls. Other girls would demurely defer to the boys when the teacher asked a question, and if I raised my hand they [female classmates] raised their eyebrows. Apparently, it just wasn't done… [In] high school, girls could be smart, but only in language arts, art, and maybe social studies. I was torn again between the choice of making friends and fitting in, and challenging myself to reach my potential.

When her family moved again and she enrolled at her new school, Amy was placed in the advanced math and science courses. She was a junior taking senior-level courses. Because the students in these advanced courses self-selected for their mutual interests in mathematics and science, Amy reflected, "I finally found 'myself' again." Although initially steered toward engineering by her counselor, Amy decided to pursue her "love of nature and biology" at the university level by majoring in wildlife biology. Her math and science skills proved helpful in the "weeder" calculus courses in this male-dominated field.

Beginning in middle school and continuing through high school, Amy's experiences are examples of how gendered learning experiences can play out and influence the development of mathematics identity. Amy's gendered experiences in mathematics classes led to a first career as a wildlife biologist and later to a second career as a middle school science and mathematics teacher. These experiences had a direct impact on Amy's beliefs about the type of mathematics teaching and learning environment that she desired for her middle school students. For example, she wanted her mathematics classroom to reflect her "gifted" mathematics class experiences. All of her students would be encouraged to be mathematicians and problem solvers. Furthermore, she voiced a strong commitment to empower all children, especially girls, to be passionate about mathematics and science. These views are directly connected to how Amy envisions her effectiveness as a mathematics teacher:

I recognize that as a teacher I will have to be careful not to teach the way I was taught in my regular classroom only, but embrace the ideas about learning I experienced in my gifted class. This is the gift I can give to all my students, and especially my girls.

Kelly Ramirez: Fourth-grade elementary teacher

Kelly Ramirez is a fourth-grade teacher at an urban elementary school. She grew up in a multiracial, bilingual (English and Spanish), working-class household. She described her elementary mathematics experiences as enjoyable. She liked solving math problems and being able to read long decimal numbers aloud in class. Her parents were supportive. However, she recalled her father's evening kitchen-table drill sessions on multiplication facts as one of the only times that she felt mathematics anxiety.

Kelly's family moved a lot. She went to three different high schools. Kelly's transitions to new schools always meant questions about her academic competencies on the basis of her Hispanic name and her family's mobility patterns:

> They usually placed me into the remedial class before I ever arrived at the school. No matter the transcripts that preceded me, full of "highly capable"–this and "gifted"–that. A child who moved nearly every year? With a Hispanic last name? They, the administrators, made swift decisions. Only after meeting my mother (the teacher) and father (the member of the clergy who was working on his PhD), would they make the switch and register me in a new class. So, very early on, I learned that proving myself academically meant that I had to overcome my name. I couldn't just compete with the Joneses. I had to excel beyond them.

Kelly rejected mathematics in high school. She excelled in her humanities and drama courses and began to stoke her passion for social justice issues in the community. She felt algebra was "stupid" and not relevant to her life. However, part of her angst came from the fact that she had to borrow a graphing calculator while her middle-class peers pulled out their shiny new TI-83s to do math problems. She completely disengaged from geometry the following year, only going to class after being punished for skipping. The saving grace of her tenth-grade year was her AP physics teacher. Impressed by her standardized test scores, he asked Kelly to take his AP physics course, where she studied mathematical concepts through physics applications. The class even went to an amusement park to ride roller coasters to prepare for the AP physics exam.

By the time Kelly transferred to her third high school, her focus was on social justice and the performing arts. At this point, mathematics "did not seem to fit." No one showed Kelly that mathematics was embedded in and relevant to her interests:

> I found joy in the self-expression of music and art and drama. Math just didn't seem to fit. But no one took the time to show me the everyday math: the fractions that came so easily when I read music, the statistics proving my points about underserved populations, or even the strict meter and syllabic count of the Bard.

A need to work with mathematics resurfaced when Kelly became manager of a nonprofit community organization that focused on supporting urban youth. Here she was in charge of budgets, statistics, and communication to funders who wanted quantifiable data.

For Kelly, both her pursuit of community activism on behalf of youth and justice and her later move to a new career as a teacher were fueled in part by mathematics learning experiences in her school and work contexts. Kelly's commitment to equity and social justice is a part of her mathematics teacher identity:

I realized that this is what kids need to know. They need to be inspired to take on the world, to fight for what is right, to express themselves in art and music … *and* they need to know the numbers. They need to be able to provide evidential, numerical proof, to balance budgets, and to fully understand the systems that they so desperately want to change. I knew I needed to make a greater impact, so I decided to become a teacher.

Socialization into or out of Mathematics: What the Autobiographies Show

The autobiographical stories of these six new teachers provide explicit examples of how the teachers themselves were socialized into or out of mathematics during their K–12 experiences and the impact of those socializing experiences on their mathematics teacher identities. Clearly, these past mathematics identities as learners directly link to their present mathematics teacher identities. Powerful experiences connected with race, class, gender, and culture shaped their view of mathematics teaching and what they want for their students' experiences. Leslie's struggle against the model minority myth prevented her from interacting with her white, middle-class peers in mathematically meaningful ways. Steve felt that the lack of cultural diversity in his environment had a negative impact on his mathematics learning experience because people from different backgrounds were absent from mathematical discussions. Amy received consistent messages from her peers suggesting that girls were not supposed to excel in mathematics—a message that contributed to her feelings of isolation in middle school and high school. Kelly's socioeconomic background was made apparent as her wealthier peers pulled out new graphing calculators while she had to borrow her calculator from the school.

Some of these teachers had powerful memories tied to specific math topics or domains that shaped their math learning identity. Some were memories of particular challenges related to mathematical topics—for example, Michael's memory of trying and failing to find alternative methods for division with fractions in an effort to prove his teacher wrong, and Shawna's experience of taking precalculus three times. Leslie's, Steve's, and Kelly's dislike of geometry had major impacts on their confidence and sense of identity as mathematics learners. Furthermore, for some of these teachers, mathematics was a critical factor in choosing a college major. Although Amy and Steve felt at ease with the mathematics that they encountered in their majors, Shawna, Leslie, and Michael changed their majors to avoid having to take mathematics.

These teachers also noted the different ways in which mathematics was made relevant—or not—in their lives. Shawna's parents provided specific everyday activities such as baking and sports to explore measurement and statistics. Michael attributed some of his mathematics skills to his participation in sports (for example, street football helped him learn multiples of seven) and reading the sports page. Kelly's physics teacher made concepts of force and motion come alive through firsthand experience with roller coasters. Two of the new teachers pointed to "missed opportunities" to make mathematics relevant. Michael's experience with construction solidified his sense that mathematics is an integral part of everyday life, although he had found it "cold and meaningless" when studying precalculus, and Kelly identified many ways to connect mathematics with aspects of her pursuit of music, theater, and social justice. Both of these teachers emphasized that making mathematics relevant to students was a key component of their math teaching vision. By telling their stories about mathematics learning, all of these teachers were able to reflect on how their own experiences as learners shaped their visions for teaching and practice, thus contributing in powerful ways to their developing mathematics teacher identities.

Power and Status of School Mathematics and Its Impact on Mathematics Teacher Identity

The math autobiographies highlight the powerful role that mathematics learning played in the lives of the six elementary and middle school teachers. All the teachers understood the importance of mathematics and how they felt when they excelled or experienced difficulties in mathematics in school. For Amy, experiences with mathematics learning fueled her passion for nature as a wildlife biologist. By contrast, Shawna, Leslie, and Steve associated their inability to do mathematics with low self-confidence and achievement.

Society commonly views mathematics as a valued and high-status subject (Gutiérrez 2010). Schools perpetuate this perspective through the gatekeeping structures associated with students' access to mathematics, such as tracking policies, reliance on standardized test scores, and specialized programs such as Advanced Placement. As we have learned from the six teachers' stories, unlike any other subject in school, mathematics has far-reaching consequences on children's academic identities and life transitions, including their economic and educational access, career decisions, and civic engagement or activism (Boaler 2002, 2008; Gutierrez 2010; Oakes 2005). Furthermore, what mathematics is has changed over time, making quantitative literacy a critical competency, essential for making sense of the data, information, and technology that are a part of our daily actions and decision making. This gives mathematics power and status that are important to understand as they relate to mathematics teacher identity.

The power and status of school mathematics often manifest themselves in decisions about what content gets taught, to which students, and by which teachers. As the narratives of the six new teachers show, what gets taught in the mathematics classroom shapes the mathematics identities of both students and teachers.

To gain a sense of the significant role that the status of mathematics plays in a math teacher identity, consider the recent "algebra for all eighth grade" policies mandated in a few states (for example, California and Minnesota) and implemented in districts across the country. Spielhagen (2011) describes the way in which a school district in the southeastern United States "detracked" the mathematics curriculum by mandating such a policy. The district implemented the policy incrementally through various stages in an effort not to overwhelm the system. Yet, the intent was to dismantle previously existing structures that blocked access to higher education for many students. Many teachers across the grade levels initially opposed the idea. The status of algebra and who had access to it became critical issues. These concerns filtered down to elementary teachers, who were feeling the pressure to "accelerate" the mathematics content for students.

According to Spielhagen, some elementary teachers claimed "that some students could not respond to such enriched experiences because they were 'not ready' for the work" (p. 37). In fact, the teachers often cited mathematical "readiness" but were unable to provide a definition on request. However, some of these teachers tied social class and family structure to readiness by citing a lack of parental support and "depressed home situations." From these teachers' perspectives, students with low socioeconomic status would be unable to gain access to or engage in the enriched mathematics experiences that the teachers believed the algebra mandate necessitated. In the words of a third-grade teacher, "Have you seen where they live? We are lucky that they get here at all" (p. 57).

So why was there such strong elementary teacher opposition to a policy intended to open up mathematics to more students? The reason was that the policy disrupted privately and publicly held notions about who should gain access to high-status mathematics, and the proposed change caused teachers to question themselves as effective teachers for particular students. No longer would algebra be reserved for an elite few. Opening up algebra meant shifting teachers' sense of their work and their knowledge about students (Drake, Spillane, and Hufferd-Ackles 2001). The deficit views of poor children and their families became apparent in the face of the demands and mandates for increased access to high-status math content, such as algebra. This change had a significant impact on the elementary teachers' identities as effective mathematics teachers and their sense of how they could best help their students.

Spielhagen's study also found that teachers criticized the algebra policy because it "lowered the bar" for a course that had been reserved for students labeled as "highly capable" and "college bound." As one middle school teacher claimed, "My goal [for the students] is AP Calculus. When I teach algebra, that's where my students are heading" (p. 55). It was hard for this middle school algebra teacher to decouple the trajectory of the "highly capable" students and the domain of algebra (precursor to AP Calculus). The policy challenged her view of the content (which she believed would no longer be rigorous), her idea of who should have access to the content (students whom she regarded as non–college bound), and thus her own identity as an effective algebra teacher. When the power and status of mathematics are challenged, the ripple effect on a teacher's mathematics teacher identity is clear.

Conclusion

Our goal in this chapter has been to highlight specific experiences and factors that shape mathematics teacher identity. The new teachers' autobiographies offer stories of supports and challenges that clearly have had a powerful impact on their own math learner identities—and, not surprisingly, a significant impact on their vision of what they want for their own students. Although some of these new teachers want to replicate what they experienced, others want to offer their future students a different, more positive experience. The importance of understanding the complex factors that contribute to a teacher's feelings, decisions, and actions related to teaching mathematics to K–8 students cannot be overstated. Experiences that teachers have in professional development or as a result of policy changes also have a significant impact on their mathematics teacher identities. Opening up access to high-status or more rigorous content can have a ripple effect on teachers' feelings of effectiveness and confidence about their likelihood of success with their students. Teaching new content with new students means a shift in thinking about practice and how to help students learn mathematics, thus seriously affecting teachers' understanding of their place in the world and their core beliefs. These experiences have an impact on our telling of our stories as math teachers—our evolving mathematics teacher identities. To promote reflection on mathematics teacher identity, we have provided a mathematics autobiography activity and a teacher identity activity at www.nctm. org/more4u. Readers can complete these activities individually or in a group setting.

DISCUSSION QUESTIONS

1. What is your mathematics learning autobiography? What aspects of your own history with learning mathematics do you think have an impact on your views about teaching mathematics? What kind of math identity do you want your students to develop in your classroom?

2. What roles did race, class, gender, culture, or language play in your math learning story? How do those experiences connect with what you have observed in your own students and their developing math identities?

3. Reflect on the new teacher stories in this chapter. What elements of these stories resonate with your own mathematics learning experience? Do you find similarities or differences across the six stories that connect with the way that you teach mathematics?

4. Think about a time when you faced a change in the mathematics curriculum (for example, a shift in policy or a new textbook). Reflect on your feelings about that change. Were you excited? Disappointed? Frustrated? What was the impact of these changes on your view of yourself as an effective math teacher?

Part 2

Rethinking Equity-Based Practices

Part 2 highlights five equity-based mathematics teaching practices that strengthen mathematical learning and cultivate positive student mathematical identities:

- *Going deep with mathematics.* Developing deep understanding of mathematics is a major goal of equity-based mathematics teaching practices (Aguirre 2009; Gutstein 2006). Lessons include high cognitive demand tasks that support and strengthen student development of the strands of mathematical proficiency, including conceptual understanding, procedural fluency, and problem solving and reasoning (National Governors Association Center for Best Practices and Council of Chief State School Officers 2010; National Research Council 2001a; Stein et al. 2000).

- *Leveraging multiple mathematical competencies.* Recognizing and positioning students' various mathematical backgrounds and competencies is a key equity-based practice (Featherstone et al. 2011; Horn 2012; Turner et al. 2012). All students have different mathematical strengths that can serve as resources for learning and teaching mathematics.

- *Affirming mathematics learners' identities.* A positive, productive mathematics learner identity contributes to the mathematical learning of a child (Berry 2008; Boaler 2002; Martin 2000, 2009; Stinson 2008). Instruction that values multiple mathematical contributions, provides multiple entry points, and promotes student participation in various ways (teams, groups, and so on) can aid the development of a student's mathematical learning identity.

- *Challenging spaces of marginality.* Traditionally, mathematics learning has been an independent and isolating experience with a focus on lecture and seatwork. Further, students who do not perform well in this traditional classroom setting are often marginalized, ignored, or positioned as "dumb" (Boaler 2002; Jackson 2009). Practices that embrace student competencies, diminish status, and value multiple mathematical contributions are essential to cultivate (Aguirre et al. 2012; Featherstone et al. 2011; Horn 2012).

- *Drawing on multiple resources of knowledge.* Equity-based teaching depends on the capacity to recognize and intentionally tap students' knowledge and experiences—mathematical, cultural, linguistic, peer, family, and community—as resources for mathematics teaching and learning. Drawing on this knowledge and experience includes helping students bridge everyday experiences to learn mathematics, capitalizing on linguistic resources to support mathematics learning, recognizing family or community mathematical practices to support mathematics learning, and finding ways to help students learn and use mathematics to solve authentic problems that affect their lives (Aguirre 2009; Aguirre et al. 2012; Civil 2007; Brenner and Moschkovich 2002; Gutiérrez 2002; Gutstein 2006; Moschkovich 1999; Simic-Mueller, Turner, and Varley 2009; Staats 2009; Turner et al. 2012; Turner and Strawhun 2007).

The preceding list is not rank-ordered; all five practices are important to use in the classroom, though not always at once or in every situation. The chapters that follow present vignettes and examples of lessons that span elementary and middle school and serve to bring these equity-based practices to life. Although each practice is discussed individually, we recognize that in the classroom these practices most often happen simultaneously and in various combinations, sometimes spontaneously.

We believe that the work of most teachers intrinsically includes elements of each of these five practices. However, tying these practices to mathematical learning and identity may be a new challenge for many. We encourage teachers to take stock of what they offer their students in relation to these practices and to build on those teaching strengths while acknowledging elements that may need additional work and making wise choices about ways to expand their use.

To assist readers with the ideas in part 2, we present a chart that summarizes the five equity-based instructional practices. The chart identifies and describes the characteristics of lessons that represent each practice. It also provides contrasting characteristics of nonrepresentative lessons, along with assessment considerations and companion questions to spark further discussion and self-reflection.

We believe that these practices are doable. But they are also intentional and complex. Attention to a few of the practices is a good start, and we encourage you to make strategic choices that will lead you to integrate all of these practices into your classrooms over time. As in part 1, the names of students, teachers, and schools that appear in the vignettes and examples are pseudonyms unless otherwise noted.

Five equity-based practices in mathematics classrooms

	A representative lesson	A nonrepresentative lesson	Assessment considerations	Questions for Reflection
Going deep with mathematics	Supports students in analyzing, comparing, justifying, and proving their solutions. Engages students in frequent debates. Presents tasks that have high cognitive demand and include multiple solution strategies and representations.	Promotes memorization without examination. Encourages students to follow procedures step by step. Presents tasks that have low cognitive demand and emphasize one solution strategy.	A task— • requires demonstration of multiple strategies or representations; • involves analysis and justification. Communication— • offers meaningful feedback that draws students' attention to "making sense" of the mathematics; • focuses on moving students' thinking forward.	How does my lesson promote mathematical analysis? How do I support students in closely examining the math concept?
Leveraging multiple mathematical competencies	Structures student collaboration to use varying math knowledge and skills to solve complex problems. Presents tasks that offer multiple entry points, allowing students with varying skills, knowledge, and levels of confidence to engage with the problem and make valuable contributions.	Promotes individual progress at specific, predetermined levels of ability. Often structures group work by ability. Presents tasks that are rigid and highly sequenced. Requires students to show mastery of skills prior to engaging in more complex problem solving.	Assessing a task— • calls for a diversified rubric and an answer key that includes math practices such as examining patterns, generalizing, abstracting, making comparisons, and specifying conditions; • requires looking for multiple ways that students demonstrate their knowledge, such as through the use of language, gestures, pictures, physical models, and concrete objects.	How do I identify and support mathematical contributions from students with different strengths and levels of confidence?

Five equity-based practices in mathematics classrooms—continued

	A representative lesson	A nonrepresentative lesson	Assessment considerations	Questions for Reflection
Affirming mathematics learners' identities	Is structured to promote student persistence and reasoning during problem solving. Encourages students to see themselves as confident problem solvers who can make valuable mathematical contributions. Assumes that mistakes and incorrect answers are sources of learning. Explicitly validates students' knowledge and experiences as math learners. Recognizes mathematical identities as multifaceted, with contributions of various kinds illustrating competence.	Is structured to emphasize speed and competition. Connects mathematical identity solely with correct answers and quickness. Explicitly discourages mistakes and immediately corrects them, often without constructive feedback. Gives ambivalent value to flexibility, reasoning, and persistence.	Communication— • focuses feedback on making sense of the mathematical idea rather than on the ratio of correct answers to the total possible; • focuses on strengths and improvements needed; • points out what is productive or problematic about a student's chosen strategy.	How do I structure my interactions with students to promote persistence with complex math problems? How do I discourage my students from linking speed with math "smartness"?

Five equity-based practices in mathematics classrooms—continued

	A representative lesson	A nonrepresentative lesson	Assessment considerations	Questions for Reflection
Challenging spaces of marginality	Centers student authentic experiences and knowledge as legitimate intellectual spaces for investigation of mathematical ideas. Positions students as sources of expertise for solving complex mathematical problems and generating math-based questions to probe a specific issue or situation. Distributes mathematics authority and presents it as interconnected among students, teacher, and text. Encourages student-to-student interaction and broad-based participation.	Disconnects student experiences and knowledge from the mathematics lesson or presupposes that students' knowledge and experiences are inconsequential to learning rigorous mathematics. Ascribes mathematics authority to the teacher or the text. Relegates complex problem solving to the end of lessons or reserves it for "more advanced" students. Segregates specific students (for example, those viewed as "low ability" or labeled as "English language learners") from the main activities. Restricts student "voice" to a few (often privileged) students.	A task— • emphasizes public discussion of mathematical ideas (whole-class, small-group, pair-share); • requires reasoning behind correct and incorrect solutions.	How do I connect my students' knowledge (in school and outside school) with the main math concept of this lesson? How do I structure a task to maximize student-generated math questions? How do I make sure that all students have opportunities to demonstrate their mathematics knowledge during the lesson?

Five equity-based practices in mathematics classrooms—continued

	A representative lesson	A nonrepresentative lesson	Assessment considerations	Questions for Reflection
Drawing on multiple resources of knowledge (math, culture, language, family, community)	Makes intentional connections to multiple knowledge resources to support mathematics learning. Uses previous mathematics knowledge as a bridge to promote new mathematics understanding. Taps mathematics knowledge and experiences related to students' culture, community, family, and history as resources. Recognizes and strengthens multiple language forms, including connections between math language and everyday language. Affirms and supports multilingualism.	Treats previous math knowledge as irrelevant or problematic (assuming, for example, "They lack skills," or "They don't know any math"). Builds on negative stereotypes of the culture, community, or family, preventing math lessons that connect with authentic knowledge and experiences of students. (Such negative stereotypes include notions like, "Many parents are laborers—they can't help their children with math," "Asian families support mathematics—that's why Asian students are so good and so quiet," and "That is not how we do division in the United States.") Discourages mathematics discourse because it is deemed too difficult for students who have not mastered standard English. Supports English as the only language spoken in the classroom.	A task involves the creation of stories or situations to solve or represent the problem. Communication offers connections to mathematical ideas that students may know but did not use in their solution or explanation.	How do I make connections with students' previous math knowledge? How do I get to know my students' backgrounds and experiences to support math learning in my classroom? How do I affirm some of my students' multilingual abilities to help them learn math? What impact have race and racism had on my mathematics lessons? How can I learn from family and community members to support my students' mathematical confidence and learning? How can I effectively communicate with families the strengths and needs of students to affirm their math identities and promote math learning?

Chapter 4

Cultivating Mathematical Agency: "He Was Suspended for Being Mexican"

An urban middle school mathematics teacher was deeply disturbed by an exchange with one of his seventh-grade students:

Mr. C:	Joaquín, where is Mario today?
Joaquín:	He ain't here. He was suspended for being Mexican.
Mr. C:	What did you say?
Joaquín:	This school is always picking on Mexicans.

Mr. C wondered whether Joaquín's claim could be true. Could the school be engaged in racial profiling of students? What could he do? Through critical reflection, confidence in his instruction, and commitment to his students as strong mathematical learners, this teacher created two standards-based data analysis mathematics lessons that engaged his middle school students in a mathematical investigation to determine whether Joaquín's claim was true.

The equity-based practices in Mr. C's mathematics classroom facilitated deep mathematical analysis (using concepts related to ratio, percent, and proportional reasoning) of an issue that strongly affected his students. Furthermore, the lessons empowered students, giving them a better understanding of how mathematics can be useful beyond the classroom walls and can promote social change. The lessons nurtured positive mathematical identity and collective mathematical agency among Mr. C's students.

The Claim: "He Was Suspended for Being Mexican"

Mr. C, a National Board Certified Teacher, had been teaching in urban elementary and middle schools for more than twelve years. A white male with a strong interest in mathematics, Mr. C had been teaching at this urban middle school for five years. Midway Middle School and its community had experienced a recent demographic shift. The school's longtime African American population had significantly decreased while three new immigrant populations—Cambodian, Mexican, and Ukrainian immigrants—were taking up residence in the nearby public housing development. The school had the highest rates of poverty (90 percent free and reduced-price lunch) and ethnic diversity (90 percent students of color) in the district. Racial and ethnic tensions were evident among the different subpopulations of the school. Furthermore, because of low test scores, this school was currently in the state's school improvement program and was under a great deal of pressure to improve student achievement, especially in mathematics.

In the face of these extensive challenges and complexities, Mr. C cared deeply about his students and was dedicated to supporting their success. This was an anchoring commitment of his instructional practice. In fact, he routinely posted the following promises in his classroom:

- I will work with you until you understand.
- I will not waste your time—every activity is tied to a learning standard.
- I will ensure that our classroom functions as a positive learning community.
- I am open to suggestions.
- I will learn along with you.

These five promises set the tone for Mr. C's mathematics classroom. Clearly, Mr. C was a teacher who valued learning (his own and his students') and was open to creating a classroom community that was supportive and positive for all.

In this context, Mr. C was seriously troubled by Joaquín's claim about the school "picking on Mexicans." He shared his concerns with one of this book's authors, Julia Aguirre, with whom he had previously collaborated on a mathematics education project. She suggested that he mathematize Joaquín's claim—in other words, use mathematics to determine whether the claim was true or false. Joaquín's statement was a *claim*, she emphasized. What was the evidence? She gave Mr. C a recent book, *Rethinking Mathematics: Teaching Social Justice by the Numbers,* by Eric Gutstein and Bob Peterson (2005). She called his attention to a short chapter on racial profiling, titled "Driving While Black/Brown." She suggested that Mr. C read this chapter and see whether he could draw some parallels to help his students analyze this claim about suspensions.

Mathematics Lessons to Evaluate the Claim

The following week, Mr. C contacted Dr. Aguirre to share his excitement about what had transpired in his seventh-grade mathematics class as a result of two lessons that he had designed and implemented. He had read the chapter and created the two lessons to investigate Joaquín's claim (activity sheets for "Midway Suspensions" [lesson 1] and

"Two Sides to Every Story" [lesson 2] are available at nctm.org/more4u). Furthermore, he had talked about the situation with his principal, who had agreed to come to the class to hear the students' conclusions. Mr. C reported that the students immediately engaged with this mathematical task, showed sustained persistence in constructing a mathematical argument, and presented their conclusions orally and in writing to the principal. The following discussion outlines the equity-based practices of Mr. C's mathematics lessons.

Going deep with mathematics

Mr. C designed two lessons that required students to determine the validity of Joaquín's statement by organizing and analyzing real data that he obtained on suspensions at Midway Middle School. In the first lesson, "Midway Suspensions," students investigated data on the general population at Midway, sorted by racial and ethnic group, along with data on the numbers of suspensions by students in these groups, and additional data on the numbers when multiple suspensions by individuals were taken into account. For the second lesson, "Two Sides to Every Story," students worked with grade-level data on numbers of students (boys and girls in different demographic groups) suspended for particular offenses. Both lessons were tied to specific grade-level state standards on data analysis. The second lesson, for example, supported the process "Solves Problems and Reasons Logically," and more specifically, the students' ability to "draw conclusions and support them using inductive and deductive reasoning."

As students began their work with "Midway Suspensions," the mathematical complexity of the activity became evident in the comparisons of ratios that it required them to make. They increased their computational fluency by representing ratios as fractions, decimals, and percentages. They generated mathematical questions related to other factors that might show the claim to be true or false. This work raised the issue of the "reasons" for suspensions at Midway. Were specific groups of students overrepresented in suspensions for a particular offense?

Mr. C designed the second lesson specifically to enable his students to explore these student-generated mathematical questions. This activity had multiple goals. It facilitated group collaboration and construction of a mathematical argument, and it included a social action component to galvanize change. Figure 4.1 presents this social action component, which proposed a letter-writing campaign using math-based arguments as a plan to make positive change in the school's learning environment.

> If your group had the power to change school policy, given your mathematical analysis, which offenses would you target to change? Why? Write a letter to the principal that describes your plan for positive change in the student learning environment at Midway. (Minimum length is 1 page.)

Fig. 4.1. Mathematizing school policy

These two activities engaged students in complex mathematical problem solving with a specific purpose that sustained interest and sparked additional mathematical questions. The lessons certainly were not the only kind of mathematical activity in this class, but going deep with the mathematics in these lessons resulted in an increased level of mathematical engagement and discourse, with students debating, computing, making mathematical comparisons and justifications, and communicating those ideas orally and in writing to support a position.

Leveraging multiple mathematical competencies

The tasks of Mr. C's lessons had multiple entry points, thus facilitating engagement by students with varying mathematical competencies. The activity sheets structured an explicit process of mathematical investigation. Collaborative teams were a norm in Mr. C's classroom, and the teamwork positioned various students as experts in this process, while underscoring the need for engagement and multiple mathematical competencies. For example, in working on the lessons on suspensions, some students with strong computational skills demonstrated to team members how to convert ratios expressed as fractions, obtained through division, into percentages. Other students with a depth of conceptual understanding pointed out which pieces of data needed to be compared and why. Mr. C structured the teams with specific roles and responsibilities that reinforced support, accountability, and progress; the roles are delineated explicitly in the activity sheet for lesson 2, "Two Sides to Every Story." He reported that his students showed a desire to work together and learn from one another. The strategies that he used recognized and leveraged different mathematical competencies to facilitate complex mathematical problem solving.

Affirming mathematics learners' identities

The second lesson, "Two Sides to Every Story," was inspired by the student-generated mathematics questions elicited in the first lesson. Students began to conjecture why members of specific groups of students were being suspended. Was there a relationship between race or ethnicity and specific offenses? Mr. C believed that his students were primed and ready to validate their questions in the second lesson. He observed them poring over the data to answer questions. Mr. C identified this enthusiasm, persistence, and analysis as evidence of his students' expanding positive mathematics learner identities. The students wanted to know more. They wanted to validate their own claims and make their case to the principal.

Although Mr. C's students had no problem sharing their opinions about issues, he believed that this was the first time that they had experienced the need for mathematics to lend support to a position—"to back up their claims." He saw their confidence increase as they prepared their arguments and wrote their letters.

Challenging spaces of marginality

Mr. C guided his students in mathematizing a specific claim that had been made by a student and reflected a larger societal reality experienced by many students of color and their families—racial profiling. These lessons also tapped into an implicit undercurrent of racial tension that had negative effects on student and community relationships. Through the opening written statement of the first lesson (see fig. 4.2), Mr. C. made his position about racism clear to his students.

> ### "He was suspended for being Mexican"
>
> Last week, I heard one of my students say this in class when describing why a friend of his was recently suspended. If this is true, I want to address the injustice immediately because I refuse to work in a racist school. Before I complain to our principal, I need to have data ready.

Fig. 4.2. Mr. C's statement on suspensions

In fact, Mr. C set up the lessons in response to racism, modeling for students the need to have "data ready" to "address the injustice" if the allegation proved to be true. This white male teacher openly used the word "racist" to describe the alleged policy, and he explicitly positioned himself against such policies and declared his commitment to changing them. He enlisted his students in helping, and they enthusiastically responded. The investigations positioned the students as mathematical experts who could give voice to an authentic concern that they experienced (Turner and Strawhun 2007). The lessons made students problem solvers and advocates for themselves and others, thus *centering*, rather than marginalizing, them as confident mathematical learners with a purpose.

Drawing on multiple resources of knowledge

A strength of Mr. C's suspension lessons was that they drew on the students' resources of knowledge to engage them in complex mathematical problem solving. The context of the lessons was an authentic issue that affected students. Their teacher gave them access to real data that required their mathematical knowledge to organize, analyze, and use to support a position. They drew on their own knowledge to generate additional conjectures about the types of offenses that might be involved. In addition, the students worked in teams, which provided peer and mathematical resources to solve these novel and complex problems. Furthermore, their letters to the principal revealed additional information about peer-to-peer interactions that were fueling negative race relations within the school, and this information prompted surveys and other strategies to promote school-community dialogues. The lessons had a positive impact on mathematical learning and identity, as well as school-community interactions.

Conclusion

Although some of the of strategies that Mr. C used were already in his teaching toolbox, these lessons extended mathematical learning and engagement in more substantive ways than Mr. C had succeeded in doing before in his classroom. For example, Mr. C believed that one of his strengths in mathematics lesson design was his ability to connect mathematics to students' lives and interests. He considered this to be a part of the multicultural emphasis in his teaching. He knew that students liked cars, had jobs, or were interested in popular culture and technology, so he often introduced mathematical ideas by using these contexts. Yet, the suspension lessons were different. They were driven by a troubling claim made by a student that related to alleged systemic racism. Although Mr. C was deeply affected by this claim, the thought of using this situation as a mathematical context for a lesson did not occur to him. Dr. Aguirre's suggestion of a related reading helped expand his repertoire of meaningful mathematical contexts:

> I think my practice reflects my tools and understanding I have at the time. When I started teaching, I was content incorporating a pretty surface-level multicultural lens. For example, I had posters up showing math from cultures around the world. Later I started thinking about accessing the diverse knowledge my students bring, but even then, it was mostly about trying to make the content of word problems more meaningful and relevant. But after reading Gutstein's critical pedagogy, I realized how much I needed another tool or model to help me think about making math meaningful and accessible to my students. Reading Gutstein's work helped.

An important dimension of Mr. C's identity as a mathematics teacher was making mathematics meaningful and accessible to his students. As Mr. C suggests, this particular dimension evolved over time from making a more superficial connection (for example, through multicultural posters) to making a more critical connection involving issues of equity and social justice.

Mr. C combined many of his successful instructional strategies—such as tying lessons to learning standards and using teams with accountability systems to monitor progress—with a new mathematical context directly tied to an authentic problem faced by many of his students of color. When asked what made these mathematics lessons different from just "good teaching," Mr. C said that he believed the lessons enabled students to tackle a serious issue that needed to be addressed within the school and community. It gave the students a sense of the importance of using mathematics to support positions, rather than just relying on opinion.

Although Mr. C knew that he took a risk in having students analyze real data related to suspensions and race, he had faith that his school's administration had no deliberate intention of engaging in racial profiling and that the principal would be open to listening to students' analyses and ideas. Mr. C's confidence in carrying out the lessons was tied to his skills as a National Board Certified Teacher, his district reputation as a strong mathematics teacher, and a positive relationship with the administration. Further, the lessons embodied Mr. C's commitment to being an "advocate for kids." He was a critical partner in his students' mathematics learning process, and he helped position his students mathematically and socially to investigate a difficult situation. He believed that the lessons had a positive impact on their sense of mathematical identity and agency. The lessons empowered students as mathematical learners, giving them confidence and a sense of purpose as they worked to gain insights and offer solutions to complex problems and make positive changes in their learning environment.

The equity-based practices of Mr. C's mathematics lessons facilitated mathematical learning, positive mathematical identity, and collective mathematical agency for students. Mr. C drew on his existing areas of expertise to create an innovative set of mathematics lessons that validated and strengthened his students' views of themselves as mathematical learners. Valuing his students' learning was already a part of Mr. C's mathematics teacher identity. He was a dedicated advocate for his students. He was committed to high expectations through mathematics standards. And he was devoted to helping students be intellectually and socially responsible for their learning.

Mr. C also faced common political and social challenges of urban schools, including accountability pressures to raise test scores and underlying racial tensions that had an impact on the learning environment of the school. His strong stance on making all lessons standards-based illustrated his commitment to high expectations within a high-stakes accountability system. At Midway, he had curricular flexibility as long as lessons were tied to standards. In addition, with these lessons, he took an explicit, public anti-racist stance. Mr. C made it clear to his students, 90 percent of whom were students of color, that he did not want to work in a "racist school." By acknowledging publicly what the claim alleged—that it charged that the school was racist—he positioned himself as an advocate for social justice in the eyes of his students.

Mr. C encouraged mathematical analysis and agency. His lessons enabled students with various types of mathematical competence to make valuable contributions. The lessons were tied to an authentic situation experienced by many students, whose knowledge and experiences they centered rather than marginalized. Students drew on their own resources—math, peer, community, and so on—to construct solutions and provide teachers and administrators with ideas for change. The lessons tapped into the expertise of students and advanced their mathematics learning. They positioned the students as possessors of mathematical resources and agency for analyzing and solving the problem related to Joaquín's claim.

DISCUSSION QUESTIONS

1. How do your curriculum and instruction cultivate mathematical agency?

2. What similarities and differences do you see between your commitment to student learning of mathematics and Mr. C's commitment? Are the outcomes of student engagement and mathematics learning in your classroom similar to those in Mr. C's classroom?

3. What kinds of authentic problems do your students face? Could you mathematize any of these problems? What are some ways in which you could identify pressing issues that students might want to change? How might you mathematize these problems?

Chapter 5

Building on Students' Strengths: The Case of Curry Green

The teachers at Rosa Parks Elementary School were having their monthly faculty meeting. This week's topic focused on mathematics—specifically, how to increase the mathematics achievement of the Title I students at the school—students considered "low performing" by law in schools with relatively high poverty rates, and all students in many of the nation's highest-poverty schools. As Ms. Davis headed back to her fourth-grade classroom, she ran into Mr. Thompson:

Mr. Thompson:	I hear you'll be getting Curry Green next week. He's really far behind. He doesn't know any of his multiplication facts. I've given him extra practice sheets for homework. They don't seem to help. He has trouble focusing and distracts the other kids with his drawing. All he wants to do is draw, all the time. It's gotten to be a real problem.
Ms. Davis:	I was thinking of starting my stations next week. Maybe I'll include multiplication array flash cards. It just might be what he needs.
Mr. Thompson:	Believe me, I know what works. He needs to know his facts. None of these Title I kids know their facts. They'll never pass algebra without understanding fractions, and they can't learn about fractions without knowing their multiplication facts.
Ms. Davis:	Knowing their multiplication facts. Is it really that simple?
Mr. Thompson:	Yes, it is. There are some skills that are prerequisites for others. Math is a linear path of skills.

The teachers in the preceding dialogue represent two opposite yet common perspectives on the teaching and learning of mathematics. Mr. Thompson believes that learning and teaching mathematics are linear processes and that a teacher's focus should be on helping students achieve mastery of a defined set of mathematical rules and procedures (Kuhs and Ball 1986). When students have acquired new knowledge, they proceed to the next set of concepts, with each concept building on the previous one. By contrast, Ms. Davis's comments reflect her belief that a student can learn and understand mathematics in multiple ways if given the opportunity. The Common Core State Standards for Mathematics (National Governors Association Center for Best Practices and Council of Chief State School Officers 2010) emphasize the importance of focusing on both conceptual and procedural knowledge. Mathematical understanding and procedural skill are equally important, and teachers can assess students' progress in developing both by using mathematical tasks of sufficient richness.

The mathematics perspective that teachers embrace has an impact on their view of their role and their effectiveness as educators (teacher identity) and subsequently governs the content that they teach and the instructional practices that they employ. Simply put, what teachers believe is important influences the decisions that they make about what content to teach, how to teach it, and, in many cases, who should receive the content (Stipek et al. 2001). In this way, teaching is no different from many other areas in life. We make decisions on the basis of what we believe.

This chapter explores the impact of the teacher's beliefs on students' learning mathematics and the role that a math teacher has in determining a student's opportunity to learn and succeed. The chapter expands the vignette about the teaching of Curry Green to explore the following teacher beliefs, which in turn shape lesson design:

1. Students should acquire conceptual as well as procedural mathematics knowledge.

2. Students' experiences and prior knowledge can be vehicles for developing conceptual and procedural knowledge.

3. Teachers have a responsibility to design learning experiences that allow each student to feel capable and successful.

Ms. Davis reflected on her mathematics instruction and constructed a lesson that incorporated many of the equity practices described in the introduction to part 2. Keep in mind that these practices often happen simultaneously in a variety of classroom interactions, making it at times challenging to identify and delineate each completely. Here we focus on the following equity-based practices that Ms. Davis used to support Curry:

- Challenging spaces of marginality
- Leveraging multiple mathematical competencies
- Going deep with mathematics
- Affirming mathematics learners' identities

The result was an engaging mathematics environment that supported Curry Green's math identity. Ms. Davis's lesson construction demonstrates how an attribute of a student's identity that has been a problem in one class can become an asset in another. The vignette illustrates that building on students' strengths can have a positive impact on the development of mathematical identity, learning, and engagement.

Mathematics Learning and Teaching at Rosa Parks Elementary

Curry Green is an African American boy in the fourth grade. He attends Rosa Parks Elementary School. The school is situated in a university town; consequently, it is very diverse ethnically, culturally, and socioeconomically. Some students have parents who are teaching for a year or so at the university, others have parents who work at the neighborhood restaurant, and still others are members of families on public assistance. The school is located in an urban district where more than 65 percent of the students are in the Title I program. The staff has undergone a recent shift, with six teachers transferring to the school from other schools as a result of budget constraints and school closures. Many of these are veteran teachers. This influx has stimulated new conversations among staff members about instructional practice and student achievement.

Although this is Curry's first year at Rosa Parks Elementary School, he already knows the school secretary very well. His teacher, Mr. Thompson, often sends him to the office. Mr. Thompson is white and has been teaching for fifteen years. He taught sixth grade at one of the middle schools in the district but because of budget cuts has been reassigned to the elementary level. Mr. Thompson loved mathematics when he was growing up. It was an easy subject for him throughout most of his schooling. He considers himself a good mathematics teacher since most of his sixth-grade students performed well on district benchmark tests. In conversation with Ms. Davis, he expressed frustration that some of the teachers didn't understand what was needed for mathematics success in the upper grades.

Ms. Davis is African American and has been teaching for six years. She regularly participates in some type of mathematics professional development in the summer to strengthen her classroom instruction. A love of mathematics is not what drew Ms. Davis to teaching. She enjoyed her school years, but she has many friends who don't feel that they did. Ms. Davis became a teacher because she wanted to be able to help other children love school and learning. It bothers her that so many of the African American and Latino students at her school struggle with math. She hasn't figured out why this is so, but she is determined to keep searching for ways to help her students achieve and be successful. In a conversation with a colleague during a professional development session, she reflected on the origin of her beliefs about mathematics:

I took just enough math to get through college and my credential program. I did well enough but by no means considered myself a math person. It wasn't until we did the square numbers activity that I realized mathematics could be understood. Who knew a square number looked like a square when drawn! Mr. Thompson and I have discussed the best way for students to learn at many faculty meetings. Yes, they do need to know their facts, but timed tests and forty-problem worksheets don't work for all kids. I used to assign worksheets with problems for homework or extra practice. I got seduced into thinking since many of my children could compute they understood multiplication. Some of my students would enter the classroom knowing their facts but didn't know how to begin to solve a multiplication application problem.

Like most teachers, Ms. Davis has seen her understanding of how to teach mathematics evolve over time. Her initial perception of what students need for success and what requirements this need imposes on instruction has also changed. She believes that all students can be successful in mathematics and that it is a teacher's responsibility to provide avenues to engage their thinking. These beliefs had a direct impact on how Ms. Davis welcomed Curry Green into her classroom, built on his strengths, and engaged him in mathematical learning.

Embracing Curry Green

Ms. Davis thought carefully about how to engage Curry Green and instill confidence in him about his ability to think and reason mathematically. Further, she designed her lessons to provide opportunities for others in the class to see Curry as a mathematically proficient student. To achieve her goals, Ms. Davis interwove and blended a number of equity-based practices.

Challenging spaces of marginality

To address Curry's expected anxiety about entering a new class belatedly in the school year, Ms. Davis provided him with a "buddy"—a partner to help him with the class routine and ease his transition to her class. She also arranged for him to be interviewed by a student and his answers to be posted on the class bulletin board. Ms. Davis has designed several welcome activities for new students. She wants each child to feel that he or she is a valued member of the classroom, so she provides opportunities for students to share their uniqueness with their peers. She believes that addressing the affective domain of students' learning is critical to their ability to gain access to the higher levels of cognitive knowledge, particularly in the case of students who have not been successful in school. Addressing a student's feelings and attitude about learning is paramount in gaining access to cognitive domain knowledge such as mathematics conceptual understanding (Blum-Anderson 1992).

After recess, Ms. Davis began her math lesson with a problem. She placed a coordinate graph activity (see fig. 5.1) on the document reader in her classroom and directed her students, "Take out your math journals."

"What's a math journal?" Curry asked. His buddy explained, "It's like our own workbook without the printed problems." Ms. Davis set the students to work on the task: "OK. Class, you have about a minute to think about the problem by yourself. When the chime rings, you can begin to talk about the problem with your partner." Ms. Davis set her phone alarm for one minute. The children copied the graph into their journals and began to write notes on the pages.

DOT AND RECTANGLE

The dot (Point A) on this graph represents a rectangle whose area is 24 square inches.

Mark two other points on the graph that represent other rectangles with area of 24 square inches.

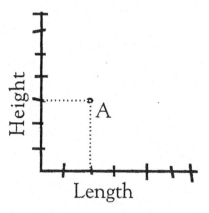

Explain why you put each dot at a particular point.
(Hint: The marks on the lines are not units of 1.)

Fig. 5.1. A coordinate graph activity presented by Ms. Davis

Curry didn't understand. "There aren't any numbers on this graph," he whispered to his buddy. His buddy responded, "We had graphs like this last week. The lines don't have to go by 1s. You can skip numbers. They just have to keep the same pattern all the way through the graph."

The alarm chimed, and Ms. Davis asked the class, "What is the problem asking you to do?" She then asked, "How do we figure out what point *A* represents? Talk with your partner and share your thoughts." The students began to talk to one another. Curry was amazed that they were allowed to talk and work with other classmates. In his other classes, he often got in trouble for talking.

After his buddy explained that each segment of the graph is a unit of 2, Curry jumped in and said, "I see. It's a rectangle, 6 by 4." Curry and his buddy located three more rectangles in the graph.

When Ms. Davis asked for volunteers to show their solutions, Curry was nervous about going up to the front of the room, but he realized that students didn't have to go forward alone. They presented in pairs, and Ms. Davis let each team decide who would speak. No one was put on the spot to explain his or her work. His anxiety level immediately went down, and he was able to listen to the team present their solutions.

Ms. Davis thanked the presenting teams and posted their solutions on the whiteboard. She said, "We are going on to another activity now. I want everyone to think about whether there's another solution we missed. We'll talk more tomorrow."

Ms. Davis used a common lesson structure, beginning with a math warm-up activity. Many teachers use this technique as a management tool, occupying students with an activity or problem while they take care of routine tasks like homework or attendance. However, a warm-up can also provide students with an opportunity to tap into prior knowledge or experiences before a new concept is introduced. A topic that students are familiar with, like coordinate graphing, provides an avenue to a new application, such as the use of an area model for multiplication. Moreover, Ms. Davis engineered opportunities for Curry to talk with a partner to verify his understanding of the mathematics in the task, a critical element in his engagement in the lesson as a new student in the class. Ms. Davis's beliefs about the benefits of student discourse contrast with the views of Mr. Thompson, in whose class Curry was made to feel marginalized because of his need to talk about mathematics.

Leveraging multiple mathematical competencies

After wrapping up the discussion of the initial problem, Ms. Davis explained the day's task: "Each of the stations today will focus on a key element for understanding and applying what we know about multiplication." Figure 5.2 shows the station activities that Ms. Davis designed to enable her students to see multiplication in different contexts (the lesson is also available at nctm.org/more4u).

Multiplication Stations		
Station 1	**Station 2**	**Station 3**
Multiplication Arrays	Why does it look like a square?	Division: A rectangle, then a little more…
[Students create a set of array cards.]	[Students build, record, and cut out models of the following facts on colored paper: 2 × 2, 3 × 3, 4 × 4, 4 × 5, 5 × 5, … 12 × 12. Then they arrange them in ways that show an increase or decrease in area.]	[Students create a rectangular array for each of the following division problems: 15/4, 64/3, 84/5; 65/7; 44/9. Then they represent each one on graph paper.]

Fig. 5.2. Ms. Davis's multiplication stations

Ms. Davis used multiple representations to assist students in developing conceptual understanding of multiplication. The sequence of tasks connected concrete, pictorial, and abstract representations of multiplication facts, allowing students to compare rectangular and square arrays and see how division with remainders compares with multiplication arrays. According to the National Research Council (2001b), "Knowledge that is taught in a variety of contexts is more likely to support flexible transfer than knowledge that is taught in a single context" (p. 17). Each station highlighted pictorial representations of multiplication (arrays), since drawing was one of Curry's strengths that Ms. Davis wanted to leverage. This design also provided the opportunity for students who had developed fluency with their facts to go deeper by exploring pictorially the inverse relationship between multiplication and division.

Going deep with mathematics

Ms. Davis called Curry's table to station 1. She explained the task: "You are going to create a set of array cards. They will help you to visualize what your multiplication facts look like and what the fact means." She asked the group, "What does 3 times 4 mean?" Carlos, Curry's buddy, answered, "Three groups of 4." Madison, a girl in the group, said, "No it doesn't. It means 12." Ms. Davis replied, "The total number of items is 12. But let's look at what it looks like."

Ms. Davis took unit cubes and built an array that had a width of 3 and a height of 4. Janelle responded, "But that also looks like 4 groups of 3 if you look at it this way." Ms. Davis replied, "You are correct, Janelle. And Carlos, you were correct, too. This multiplication array, or rectangle, can be represented in two ways. We refer to that fact as the *commutative property of multiplication*. The order of the two numbers doesn't affect their product, or answer. Let's draw them on our index cards."

Curry sketched his arrays with a perspective view of the cubes. Ms. Davis looked over in amazement at Curry's drawing. He had drawn a 3-dimensional representation of the array. When he saw her facial expression, he quickly erased it and said, "I'm sorry." Ms. Davis replied, "Curry. No. Don't erase it. That's exactly how it looks from an overhead perspective. I am going to draw a 2-dimensional representation because it's easier for me to draw."

Ms. Davis stated, "We will also write the related division equation. Who knows what that would be?" Curry looked at the array a minute and replied quietly, "Twelve divided by 4 equals 3?" Ms. Davis affirmed his answer, "Yes, that is correct." Curry smiled. Ms. Davis followed up with another question, "What's another division equation?" Curry responded tentatively, "Twelve divided by 3 equals 4?" Ms. Davis affirmed his response again: "Excellent! So our array gives us information about both the multiplication and division fact. Let's try a few more." Figure 5.3 illustrates the students' work with Ms. Davis.

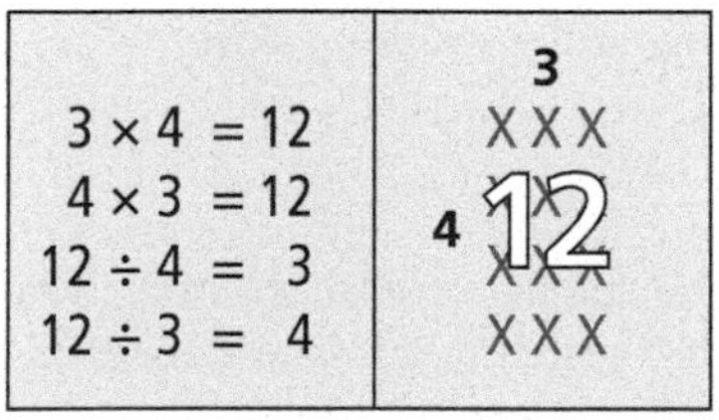

Fig. 5.3. Multiplication and division activity in Ms. Davis's class

Station 1 allowed multiple mathematical competencies to be showcased. The students offered two responses to Ms. Davis's initial question, "What does 3 times 4 mean?" Ms. Davis validated both responses and capitalized on the opportunity to show how they were related through multiple representations, the commutative property of multiplication, and the inverse relationship between multiplication and division in fact families. Curry's participation demonstrated that he was making important learning connections. He was also able to recognize and recall multiplication and division facts while working on this task—a competency that he had been unable to demonstrate in his previous class.

Affirming mathematics learners' identities

Ms. Davis's students continued to work with their partners to create sets of array cards for the 8 and 9 times tables. Curry was surprised when the bell rang for lunch. On the way out, Ms. Davis asked Curry how he had liked working in stations that morning. She acknowledged how challenging making the transition to a new classroom can be and told him he had worked well with his partner in completing the cards. She said, "I know it can be tough walking into the middle of a math lesson in a new class."

Curry responded, "It was OK. It didn't seem like math class to me. It's really different than in Mr. Thompson's room. We get to talk *and* draw." Ms. Davis explained that learning to visualize problems was a mathematics problem-solving skill that everyone needs to acquire. "Some students naturally process information that way, but for others it is helpful to talk through their math problems to understand what's needed for a solution. There isn't a right or wrong way to think, just different ways." Curry thought for a minute and then said, "I always thought I was the dumb one in class. I just didn't get it sometimes, especially in math. It's so hard to remember all those numbers and rules." Ms. Davis agreed. "It's easier to memorize when you understand what you're memorizing. That's why we always strive for understanding in our class, Curry. It makes us much better mathematicians." Curry asked, "Does that mean no timed tests?" She responded, "No. We all learn at different paces. Speed will come in time. Don't worry." Curry smiled and said, "Thanks, Ms. Davis."

This poignant exchange between Curry and Ms. Davis emphasizes how the mathematics identities of students can be shaped and reshaped through positive mathematics learning experiences. Ms. Davis's responses to Curry affirmed his developing positive mathematical identity. The view that she provided of what it means to learn and be successful in mathematics was broader than the perspectives that Curry had previously encountered. Ms. Davis helped Curry readjust his perception of what it means to be "good at math" and gave him a new vision that included a path potentially leading to both conceptual understanding and procedural skill.

Conclusion

Many third- and fourth-grade teachers regard mastery of multiplication facts as a curricular cornerstone for their students. However, for students, mastering the facts and conceptually understanding what multiplication means are two different things. It is critical to develop proficiency in both. This can be particularly true for students of color, who historically have had limited access to cognitively demanding tasks and courses. Focusing on timed mastery can lead to negative dispositions toward mathematics (National Research Council 2001b).

Mr. Thompson and Ms. Davis, the two teachers portrayed in this chapter, display very different perspectives on mathematics proficiency and the knowledge and skills necessary to achieve mathematics success. Their differences had a significant impact on Curry Green's mathematical experience and his developing mathematical identity. Mr. Thompson's personal experiences as a mathematics learner and educator had shaped his opinion of the criteria for math success and his views regarding teaching. When assigned to a new school and grade level, he designed his instruction on the basis of these beliefs and became frustrated because he was not able to achieve the same level of success in his new surroundings that he had attained in his old ones. When teachers inherit a class of students who struggle with mathematics or have been identified as low achievers, too often they assume that procedural, low-level remediation is most appropriate. Mr. Thompson quickly began to look at what his students *lacked* and what changes they needed to make, rather than to reflect on his *own* beliefs about mathematics learning and teaching.

Ms. Davis, on the other hand, was guided in her teaching by a belief that learning mathematics is a sense-making process and that the teacher must create a classroom environment where children feel included and their uniqueness is honored. Curry Green was a student not unlike many students in our schools today. He was a bright African American boy who had not experienced a great deal of success in mathematics. Ms. Davis embraced the multiple identities that he brought to her classroom. She embedded equitable teaching practices in the lessons that she designed to ensure that those lessons would tap into her students' mathematical strengths and enable them to see themselves as successful mathematics learners.

DISCUSSION QUESTIONS

1. Ms. Davis's and Mr. Thompson's professional and personal experiences shaped their conflicting perspectives and beliefs about the necessary elements for success in mathematics. They also had different views of Curry Green as a mathematics learner. Reflecting on your own experiences, what do you believe are the critical components for mathematics success? How are these reflected in your instructional practice? Do Ms. Davis's views or Mr. Thompson's views resonate with your own beliefs and experiences?

2. How might you support students like Curry, who might have a negative mathematical identity but nevertheless have positive identities in other areas of their life?

3. Ms. Davis leveraged Curry's strengths as an artist to deepen his understanding of multiplication and fact fluency. In what ways have your math lessons tapped into a student's strengths?

DISCUSSION QUESTIONS—*CONTINUED*

4. Statistics show that students of color, second language learners, and learners from families of lower socioeconomic status often receive mathematics instruction that is predominantly procedural and skill-based. What conversations have you had with colleagues at your school site on differentiated instruction for specific groups of students?

Chapter 6

Mathematics Assessment within Equity-Based Practices

Assessment is a multifaceted *process*.

Mathematical competence is complex and multidimensional.... What a student knows and is able to do does not simply add up to a larger and larger amount as days go by. Progress is not a unilateral leap forward. So I would need to teach my students to see competence as multifaceted and complex. (Lampert 2001, p. 330)

The aim of the process of assessment is "gathering evidence about a student's knowledge of, ability to use, and disposition toward mathematics and making inferences from that evidence for a variety of purposes" (NCTM 1995, p. 3). Because mathematical competence is complex and multidimensional, tools to assess mathematical competence must be equally multifaceted to capture a child's mathematical growth and progress accurately. However, facilitating teachers' understanding of students' mathematical learning is not the only essential purpose of assessment. Communication of their learning progress to various stakeholders, especially the students themselves and their families, along with using that information to promote learning, is equally important.

Because no two students, teachers, classroom communities, or schools are alike, we do not attempt to offer a prescription for developing richer assessment tasks. Instead, we provide common assessment scenarios that new and experienced teachers will recognize, including unit assessments, timed fluency tests, and problem-solving tasks, and we offer ways to rethink *routine assessment practices*. We agree that a fundamental principle of assessment is that it must first promote student learning (Black et al. 2004; Miller-Jones and Greer 2009). We extend this fundamental principle of assessment to include affirming and strengthening positive mathematics identities among students.

This chapter discusses specific ways that teachers can rethink their routine assessment practices in light of the five equity-based practices described in this book. First, we illustrate ways to provide *meaningful feedback* to students about their learning. We believe that the types of feedback that students receive can have a tremendous impact on the progress of their mathematical learning and their conceptions of themselves as mathematics learners. Next, we discuss some of the explicit ways in which teachers can recognize and tap into various forms of background knowledge and resources that students bring to assessment tasks. Consideration of these resources can serve as learning opportunities for teachers to enhance their own understanding of what students know and can do. We encourage teachers to reflect deeply on the strategies discussed in this chapter and then take action to enhance their equity-based assessment practices and improve the mathematics learning and identity development of their students.

Rethinking Assessment by Providing Meaningful Feedback

Think about the ways that students' progress, or lack of progress, in mathematics is conveyed to them. What do students see on chapter tests or homework that come back to them? A score? A percentage? Smiley faces? Check marks? Research has documented that feedback from assessments about ability and competence often has a negative impact on students, especially those from historically marginalized groups (Black et al. 2004). In particular, feedback tends to accentuate what students do not know and cannot do, thus leading them to believe that they are "not smart," lack ability, or cannot learn.

The types of feedback that students receive on assessments can contribute to their developing identities as mathematics learners. Feedback has the power to determine whether children see themselves as mathematically proficient. We encourage more holistic, positive, and specific approaches that give meaningful feedback to students with different levels of understanding. These approaches include focusing students' attention on making sense of mathematics, affirming evidence of mathematical progress (such as innovative strategies and correct answers and procedures), and providing students with opportunities to grow mathematically without sacrificing their mathematical confidence.

To illustrate models of meaningful feedback, we showcase examples of student work along with feedback that demonstrates a range of mathematical understanding (full, partial, emergent). Our purpose here is to provide specific ways in which teachers can give students meaningful feedback that offers strategic guidance for making further mathematical progress. We believe that all students, including those identified as high achievers, need specific feedback to affirm what they do know and can do, as well as feedback that will help orient and move their mathematical thinking forward.

Performance-based assessment task: Floors 4 U

We present three examples of work by sixth-grade students on a performance-based assessment task called "Floors 4 U" (Mathematics Assessment Resource Service 2010). The task assesses knowledge of area and perimeter. The real-world context of the problem is designing and measuring carpet, and students are asked to determine the amount of red carpet needed for a triangular design in a square carpet that is 8 yards by 8 yards. The student work in figure 6.1 shows the picture provided of the carpet, with the specific dimensions noted.

The figure shows three examples of student work illustrating full, partial, and emergent understanding, as measured by the evaluation rubric. The figure shows written models of meaningful feedback and how that feedback can be linked to the equity-based practices stressed in this book, particularly *going deep with mathematics* and *affirming mathematics learners' identities*.

The aim of the feedback is to give strategic guidance to students about which aspects of their mathematical explanations are praiseworthy and which need further development (Lampert 2001). This is the core of equity-based assessment practice and can be carried out with respect to a student's level of current understanding. The feedback consists of short sentences designed to draw students' attention to specific aspects of their solutions. Orienting students' attention to productive and problematic understandings positions teachers to offer explicit guidance about what mathematical ideas to revisit and think about more deeply. This guidance is often impossible to provide with check marks or smiley faces. Further, incorporating opportunities to revise work on the basis of meaningful feedback enables students to move forward in their mathematics understanding in productive ways that can keep their positive mathematics learner identities intact.

We recognize that providing this type of feedback can be time-intensive initially. However, we encourage teachers to find ways to incorporate more specific feedback as an ongoing pedagogical practice. One possibility is to select a specific test or one or two problems on a test for more detailed feedback. Collaboratively creating feedback questions is also an excellent professional development activity for grade-level colleagues. Moreover, we recommend engaging students in explicit discussion—one-on-one or in small-group or whole-class settings—after offering more detailed feedback that enables students to make sense of their progress on an assessment.

Next, we explore additional ways to give meaningful feedback in routine assessment contexts such as curriculum unit tests and fluency tests. We invite you to rethink the ways in which you communicate progress to students in relation to the models presented above and the five equity-based practices.

Unit tests

Figures 6.2 and 6.3 (see pages 73 and 74) show examples of feedback on two students' work in response to a second-grade assessment item for an Everyday Mathematics lesson focused on number and operation (University of Chicago School Mathematics Project 2007). The item uses a domino representation of two sets of dots in assessing students' knowledge of fact families. Students A and B were in the same school but had different teachers. Both students were given an N (not adequate progress) for their work on this assessment item. Figure 6.2 presents student A's work and her teacher's feedback.

Student 1: Jed (full understanding)	Example of meaningful feedback	Links to equity-based strategies
2. The leisure center wants the carpet for this square floor to be in two different colors like the diagram. The floor is 8 yards long and 8 yards wide. How much red carpet will be needed? _____ square yards Explain how you figured this out. First I multiplied 8×8 which = 64, then I knew red is $\frac{1}{2}$ and the 2 blues are $\frac{1}{4}$ so add them together and you get $\frac{1}{2}$ so then I divided 64 by 2 and got 32.	Clear use of your fraction knowledge to explain how triangles are related to the whole and why you divided the area of the square by 2. Calculations are correct. How did you know that the red triangle equaled 1/2? What do you know about the relationship of triangles and squares that makes you think the red triangle is 1/2 and the blue triangles are each 1/4?	• *Going deep with mathematics* • *Affirming mathematics learners' identities* Jed's answer is correct, his multiplication and division calculations are correct, and he shows clear understanding of part-whole relationships in fractions. The feedback goes beyond phrases like "good job" and directly addresses strengths of Jed's explanation. By doing so, it affirms his identity as a math learner. To deepen Jed's mathematics understanding, the feedback includes questions that focus his attention on examining underlying mathematical structures of the problem. Specifically, the feedback asks him to be more explicit about how he determined the fractional amounts and how those fractions connect with the relationship between squares and triangles.

Fig. 6.1. Examples of meaningful feedback on three students' work on a performance-based assessment task

Student 2: Desiree (partial understanding)	Example of meaningful feedback	Links to equity-based strategies
2. The leisure center wants the carpet for this square floor to be in two different colors like the diagram. The floor is 8 yards long and 8 yards wide. How much red carpet will be needed? ___32___ square yards Explain how you figured this out. 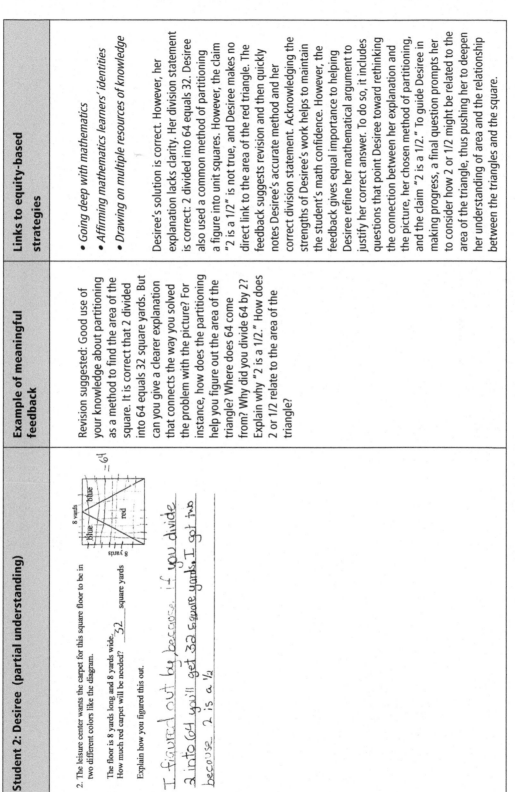 I figured out by because if you divide 2 into 64 you'll get 32 square yards, I got two because 2 is a 1/2	Revision suggested: Good use of your knowledge about partitioning as a method to find the area of the square. It is correct that 2 divided into 64 equals 32 square yards. But can you give a clearer explanation that connects the way you solved the problem with the picture? For instance, how does the partitioning help you figure out the area of the triangle? Where does 64 come from? Why did you divide 64 by 2? Explain why "2 is a 1/2." How does 2 or 1/2 relate to the area of the triangle?	• *Going deep with mathematics* • *Affirming mathematics learners' identities* • *Drawing on multiple resources of knowledge* Desiree's solution is correct. However, her explanation lacks clarity. Her division statement is correct: 2 divided into 64 equals 32. Desiree also used a common method of partitioning a figure into unit squares. However, the claim "2 is a 1/2" is not true, and Desiree makes no direct link to the area of the red triangle. The feedback suggests revision and then quickly notes Desiree's accurate method and her correct division statement. Acknowledging the strengths of Desiree's work helps to maintain the student's math confidence. However, the feedback gives equal importance to helping Desiree refine her mathematical argument to justify her correct answer. To do so, it includes questions that point Desiree toward rethinking the connection between her explanation and the picture, her chosen method of partitioning, and the claim "2 is a 1/2." To guide Desiree in making progress, a final question prompts her to consider how 2 or 1/2 might be related to the area of the triangle, thus pushing her to deepen her understanding of area and the relationship between the triangles and the square.

Fig. 6.1. Examples of meaningful feedback on three students' work on a performance-based assessment task, *continued*

Student 3: José (emergent understanding)	Example of meaningful feedback	Links to equity-based strategies
2. The leisure center wants the carpet for this square floor to be in two different colors like the diagram. The floor is 8 yards long and 8 yards wide. How much red carpet will be needed? _39_ square yards Explain how you figured this out. I found the area first and made squares on the triangle and counted them, and it was 39	Revision needed: Good partitioning model for understanding the area of the square. 64 square yards is the area of the square. But how did you get 39 square yards in the red triangle? Your counting strategy is not clear. How are the areas of the red and blue triangles related to the area of the square in this picture? What part of the whole square do they represent? How could you use what you know about the area of a square to help you find the area of the red triangle?	• *Going deep with mathematics* • *Affirming mathematics learners' identities* • *Drawing on multiple resources of knowledge* José's answer is incorrect, and his explanation is limited. The feedback begins by suggesting revision and immediately follows this suggestion by a positive statement that affirms José's clear use of an appropriate mathematics strategy to find the area of a square—partitioning the figure and counting the unit squares. However, this partitioning strategy can be limiting with more complex figures, particularly with triangles, and in this case, the strategy produced a miscount of unit squares. The feedback acknowledges the strategy and indicates how it is problematic. To deepen José's mathematics understanding, the comments focus his attention on the relationship between the triangles and the square and on part-whole relationships. The feedback is designed to connect to other mathematical knowledge about part-whole relationships and areas of specific shapes that José may have but did not use in this problem. This feedback can help guide his revision.

Fig. 6.1. Examples of meaningful feedback on three students' work on a performance-based assessment task, *continued*

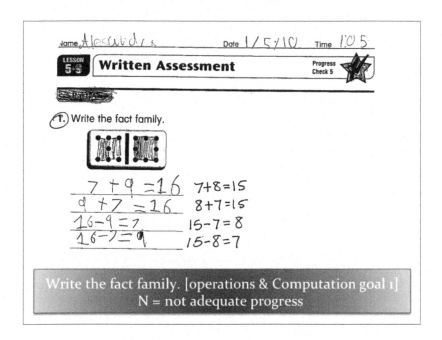

Fig. 6.2. Sample work from student A and teacher feedback

As the figure shows, the teacher's feedback on this second grader's work is very straightforward. The correct four-fact family connected with the domino representation is written next to the student's four-fact family number sentences. However, the feedback makes no explicit connection between the student's solution and the teacher's correction other than their close proximity. One issue to consider is whether student A does show knowledge of fact families. She provides four mathematically correct number sentences, consisting of two addition sentences and two subtraction sentences, which include the numbers 7, 9, and 16. Clearly, she did not accurately "count" the number of dots on the right-hand side of the domino. If we think about ways to draw this student's attention to the mathematics to make sense of it, what question or comment (written or oral) could we offer to extend her understandings about fact families?

One way might be to acknowledge student A's demonstration of understanding of a fact family. Using the approach illustrated in figure 6.1, the teacher could acknowledge the student's counting error but write something like, "Good use of fact family addition and subtraction equations for the numbers 7, 9, and 16." Then the teacher could follow up by drawing an arrow connecting the fact family written by the student and the domino with a question such as, "Do these match?" In this way, the teacher could recognize this student's growing understanding of fact families while drawing her attention to the discrepancy between the pictorial representation in the domino and the number sentences depicting that representation.

Consider the second example involving a student's work on the same problem with feedback from a different teacher. Student B's work appears along with teacher feedback in figure 6.3.

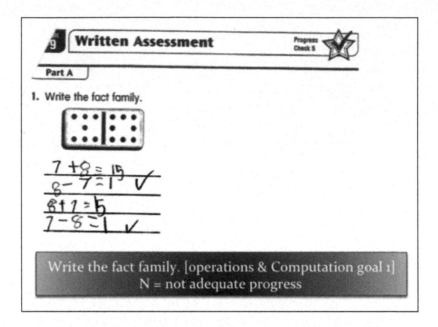

Fig. 6.3. Sample work from student B and teacher feedback

In this case, the teacher conveys the feedback through check marks on two of the four number sentences. The check marks are attached to two subtraction number sentences. Although one subtraction sentence (8 − 7 = 1) is mathematically correct, it is not a fact family number sentence that reflects the domino representation. The second subtraction sentence is clearly incorrect. Does this student demonstrate knowledge of fact families? How does the feedback assist him in deepening his math understanding of number relationships by working with fact families?

If we focus on the primary aims of promoting student learning and positive mathematics identities, this kind of feedback gives us pause. Clearly, this student's understanding is still emerging. Although the addition equations are correct and match the representation, the subtraction equations tell a different story, raising questions about the student's understanding of number relationships. Meaningful feedback would require more specificity in this case to deepen this student's mathematical understanding. An important point to make with this student is that the addition equations need to "match" the representation. However, focusing in on the subtraction equations, we might acknowledge the correctness of the first subtraction, but point out that the subtraction equation does not match the domino picture. We could write something like, "Almost! The addition equations of the fact family match the domino. But does the subtraction equation match? Does 8 − 7 = 1 match the picture?" Then the teacher could draw an arrow to the picture and list the specific numbers (7, 8, 15) that should be in all four equations.

These two examples of the same summative assessment item are designed to promote reflection about how feedback is often given to students, and by extension, to their parents, who might be reviewing the test results. The goal here is to provide feedback that promotes deeper mathematical understanding, acknowledges what the child did correctly, and guides the child's attention to misunderstandings that need to be addressed. Teacher feedback plays a crucial role in the process.

Fact fluency assessments

Michael Allen, a fifth-grade elementary teacher, is one of the six new teachers whose mathematics autobiographies are presented in chapter 3. Michael describes his early mathematics experiences:

> My earliest math memories are of timed fact fluency tests in third grade. I remember that I was disappointed to not be one of the fastest in my class. However, I also remember being relieved that I was not one of the slowest either.

Although Michael is a teacher now, his earliest memories of mathematics learning focus on a widely used assessment for multiplication and division math facts—also known as "timings"—short tests with 20–60 problems of similar type that students are expected to complete within a short period of time (1–3 minutes). What is important to note about Michael's words is the relationship of these timings to his identity as a mathematics learner. Being "slow" or "fast" was determined by this kind of assessment and brought both disappointment and relief to Michael as a young student.

Because of their widespread use, fact fluency timings and the role that they play in students' mathematical learning and mathematics identities are important to think about. Students do need to develop robust forms of procedural fluency that emphasize efficiency, accuracy, and flexibility (Russell 2000). Although these assessments may work to develop efficiency and accuracy through rote memorization, they do little to promote flexibility and understanding of procedures (National Research Council 2001a). Furthermore, as reflected in Michael's comment, speed is connected to status and "smartness" in mathematics. Being slow puts students at risk for marginalization. Thus, although the intent of such assessments is to strengthen a specific mathematical skill, the consequences for students' mathematics identities are far-reaching and need to be considered.

Figure 6.4 provides an example of a typical way in which teachers construct and score such timings. Feedback is usually given in the form of a fraction: total number of correct answers over total number of problems (in this case, $^{20}/_{26}$). Incorrect answers are noted by a check mark. The time taken to complete the task is also noted in minutes and seconds (1:52).

This form of feedback—check marks—emphasizes the mistakes made. In some cases, students might have to take this test over until they reach 100 percent accuracy before moving on to the next fact timing. Over time, if students continue to struggle with accuracy or efficiency (by not completing all the problems in a given timing), this process can diminish their confidence as mathematics learners.

How can feedback on timings be made more meaningful? One approach is to do a close analysis of the student's work, looking for specific patterns in correct and incorrect answers. Are there specific consistencies or inconsistencies? Here we extend traditional error analysis (Ashlock 2002) to a more balanced "strength-need" analysis of the student's work to address his or her mathematical learning progress more effectively.

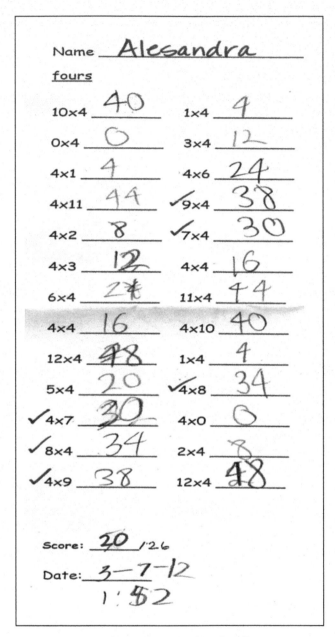

Fig. 6.4. Fourth-grade multiplication fluency test

In the work displayed in figure 6.4, the student is consistently correct in her use of the following 4 facts:

$$4 \times 0, \quad 4 \times 1, \quad 4 \times 2, \quad 4 \times 3, \quad 4 \times 4, \quad 4 \times 5, \quad 4 \times 10, \quad 4 \times 11, \quad 4 \times 12$$

Furthermore, the student appears to understand the commutative property of multiplication (that is, $a \times b = b \times a$) in the 4 facts as well. Emphasizing the four facts that the student has mastered will help the student—and the parents who assist the student at home—to be more strategic about working on the facts that still need mastery. The work in figure 6.4 also reveals a group of 4 facts that still needs work:

$$4 \times 6, \quad 4 \times 7, \quad 4 \times 8, \quad \text{and} \quad 4 \times 9.$$

Although the feedback provided by check marks is immediate, it is not always meaningful, indicating how students can strengthen their mastery of multiplication facts. One way to give such feedback is to focus students' attention on the meanings, interpretations, and models of multiplication and their relationships to known facts and bridging from the facts that students do know to those that they have yet to learn. Written feedback that draws student attention in this way on timed tests on "4s" could include statements such as the following:

- Almost there! You've got most of your 4 facts down. Let's work on 4×6, 4×7, 4×8, and 4×9. Let's bridge! How can the facts $4 \times 1 = 4$ and $4 \times 10 = 40$ help you remember 4×9? How can $4 \times 5 = 20$ help you remember 4×6?

- Close! We just have to work on the middle facts (4×6, 4×7, 4×8, 4×9). What is the relationship between 4×4 and 4×8? Use our doubling strategy. How are 4×3 and 4×6 related? You can do this!

The key here is to provide meaningful feedback to deepen students' understandings and to help them connect their previously mastered knowledge with what they still need to learn. Focusing the feedback on mathematical properties such as the distributive property and strategies like doubling can help students make these connections. Further, this type of written feedback is positive, encouraging, and strategic. It affirms the multiplication facts that students know, suggests ways to bridge to facts that they have yet learn, and affirms their identities as mathematical learners moving forward.

Rethinking Assessment to Engage Multiple Knowledge Resources

During mathematics lessons, teachers can use assessment to recognize and engage the multiple forms of background knowledge and resources that students bring to mathematical problem-solving situations. They can use these to develop more holistic understandings of what their students know and can do. The fifth equity-based practice specifically focuses on *drawing on multiple resources of knowledge,* including mathematical, cultural, linguistic, family, and community resources. These resources are grounded in the social realities and experiences of students and can contribute to their learning and the development of positive mathematics identities. We argue that teachers can learn more about how students are making sense of mathematical ideas by paying attention to these resources as they are expressed and communicated by students in their written and oral presentations of their work. We discuss two examples that offer ways that teachers can rethink their assessment practices and maximize their opportunities to learn more about the resources that students bring to bear on math problems.

Valentine Exchange activity

During a fourth-grade math lesson, the teacher, Mrs. Olivas, carefully posed a series of questions that asked students to determine the number of valentines exchanged among the twenty-four students in the class at the recent Valentine's Day party. Each student had exchanged one valentine with every other student. To launch the lesson, Mrs. Olivas posed simple scenarios involving exchanges among two people, three people, and four people, asking her fourth graders to predict a solution and then model the valentine exchanges physically to verify the predictions. Her launch of the lesson was limited by her use of only one valentine when modeling the exchange. However, her students developed and clarified their understanding by modeling the exchange that had occurred previously at the party. (The teacher's and students' real names are used in this example; edited footage of the Valentine Exchange lesson [video 42] appears at http://www.learner.org /resources/series32.html?pop=yes&pid=910.)

Figure 6.5 shows a re-creation of a drawing made on the board by Armando, a Spanish-dominant fourth grader in Mrs. Olivas's class. This drawing is a pictorial representation of Armando's solution to the question that Mrs. Olivas posed orally: "If there were four people that exchanged valentines, how many valentines would be exchanged?"

Fig. 6.5. A re-creation of Armando's blackboard drawing

While Armando explained his solution in Spanish, he pointed to the different combinations represented in the rectangles and counted in Spanish: "uno, dos, tres, cuatro, cinco, seis, siete, ocho, nueve, diez, once, doce," thus demonstrating that there would be twelve exchanges among four people. The four people in the picture represented three classmates—Denry (D), Chelsea (C), and Gina (G)) and the teacher, Mrs. Olivas (O)—who had just physically modeled the exchange of valentines.

Armando's representation provided Mrs. Olivas with a clearer understanding of his mathematical thinking, including the resources that he brought to bear in this explanation. His picture modeled different mathematical features of the situation—the people involved and the different combinations of card exchanges. He accounted for each person exchanging a card with another person by recording the initials of each person involved in an exchange in a rectangle below the pictured person. In this lesson, English was the primary language of instruction. But Armando's explanation combined his visual representation with gestures, such as pointing to the combination rectangles, to convey his mathematical understanding of this problem. By inviting Armando to explain his solution in his first language, as well as through pictures and gestures, Mrs. Olivas enabled Armando to make a valuable contribution to the mathematical discussion that benefited his English-only and bilingual peers (Aguirre et al. 2012; Moschkovich 1999). An ELL student, Armando was not relegated to the margins or ignored during this lesson. He participated as a legitimate classroom member, offered an alternative reasoning strategy and a representation to solve the problem, and received affirmation of his mathematics identity along with his linguistic identity.

Armando's solution provided solid evidence of a reasoning strategy that could be leveraged to further develop skills in pattern identification and generalization to determine how many valentines would be exchanged in larger groups, such as the class of twenty-four students, the entire fourth grade, or any number of people. In the future, Mrs. Olivas could offer further support for Armando's mathematical understanding by helping him recognize the limitation of using pictures as an efficient representation for valentine exchange combinations with larger groups of people. At the same time, she could use his representation as a reference to help him notice a pattern among the cards exchanged: each person gives a card to someone else except for himself or herself (that is, the picture has no rectangles with identical initials, such as D, D). Helping Armando see the strengths and limitations of his solution is an equity-based assessment strategy that can deepen his mathematical understanding.

Bus Pass problem

Figure 6.6 presents a "best buy" problem that was given to students in a predominantly African American urban middle school (Tate 1994). Many students reasoned about and solved the problem in a way that test designers did not anticipate.

Bus Pass Problem

It costs $1.50 each way to ride the bus between home and work. A weekly pass is $16. Which is the better deal, paying the daily fare or buying the weekly pass?

Fig. 6.6. The Bus Pass problem

The assumption of the district's test designers was that students who solved the problem correctly would choose to pay the daily fare. When a large number of students answered the problem "incorrectly," teachers discussed reasons for this outcome with their students. The teachers discovered that the assessment item was based on a particular set of assumptions that privileged students accustomed to thinking in terms of a 9–5 weekday work schedule and people having only one job. However, many African American students solved the mathematical problem under a different set of assumptions based on their daily lives and social realities.

When the teachers asked some African American students to explain their choice of the weekly bus pass, the students indicated that the weekly pass was the better option because it could be used in a variety of ways that were work and non-work related. It could also be used on weekends or by other family members. The African American students made accurate mathematical computations in the context of the specific scenario; however, their ultimate selection of the weekly bus pass over the individual daily fare as the better deal was based on different assumptions, grounded in their home and community experiences.

Although many arguments can be made about why the Bus Pass problem is or is not a good assessment question, we focus here on the *learning opportunities* that such a question provides for teachers, enabling them to reflect on the equity-based practices promoted in this book. The important point in this context is that mathematical understanding is not disconnected from students' social realities. In fact, students with different backgrounds and experiences draw on these to make sense of ideas and problem-solving situations. The Bus Pass problem uncovered the different mathematical assumptions made by the students and the test designers, grounded, perhaps, in different social realities. It is important to recognize and engage these kinds of assumptions in the classroom to get a better understanding of what students know and can do.

For example, after closely examining student work and the responses that differed from the solution presumed to be correct, teachers might have asked the following question as a way to probe the mathematics more deeply with their students: "What mathematics skills, concepts, and thinking strategies did you actually use to *derive* your solutions to the problem?" In the Bus Pass scenario, students would have had to demonstrate computational accuracy and fluency in determining the total amount paid, based on individual fares. But because many of the students reasoned about the possibility of multiple uses, the problem also allowed students to demonstrate skills in strategic reasoning and problem solving.

The assessment item also showcases the ways in which students draw on their everyday and cultural experiences to make sense of mathematics problems that are presented in school. This kind of assessment task can open up opportunities to leverage multiple mathematical competencies and make transparent the mathematical and background resources that students draw on to solve the problem. Moreover, given that students are likely to be personally invested in their solutions, they may be more likely to share and justify their thinking out loud and give meaning to the mathematics that they used to generate the solutions. In doing so, students recognize that their mathematical contributions are valued, and thus the spaces in which students are marginalized may shrink.

If students are struggling to generate meaningful solutions on their own, teachers can ask them to build on one another's partial solutions. This activity could help to create classroom environments where the teacher and students can leverage one another's multiple competencies. When students generate various solutions to a problem, as in the case of the Bus Pass problem, teachers can use this situation as an opportunity not only to confirm the possibility of multiple solutions but also to explore alternative strategies, assumptions, and solutions generated by students. By acknowledging multiple student solutions and thinking processes, teachers can positively affirm students' mathematical identities, showing that equally valid solutions can be generated by different students, thus affirming all students as powerful "doers of mathematics" and changing the nature of mathematics classrooms from places where "smart" and "not smart" student mathematics identities emerge.

The Valentine Exchange lesson and the Bus Pass problem highlight ways in which teachers can rethink assessment to take advantage of the mathematical resources that students bring to mathematical problem solving. It is important to remain alert for these mathematical resources when they emerge in a lesson and recognize and engage them as essential sources of information for understanding what students know and can do. Paying close attention to how social realities inform mathematical assumptions and shape learning will benefit instructional decision making that supports students' mathematical progress and strengthens their mathematical identities.

Conclusion

Assessment is a key component of all teachers' instructional practice. It can be a vital tool, aimed primarily at promoting learning and positive mathematics identities in students. Providing meaningful feedback enables students to make sense of their current and future mathematical progress. Engaging the multiple forms of knowledge and background resources that students bring to the classroom and using them to help students gain a better understanding of mathematics and extend their mathematical progress and confidence are fundamental to equity-based practice. Finding ways that encourage students to make sense of the mathematics, draw on their previous knowledge, and affirm their existing competencies should be key goals for all teachers.

DISCUSSION QUESTIONS

1. How do you communicate mathematical accomplishment or progress to students?

2. Select a sample of student work. On the basis of some of the examples of meaningful feedback provided in this chapter, decide what kinds of comments you can write to extend the student's mathematical thinking and preserve a positive mathematics identity.

3. In what ways have you noticed students using their everyday lives and experiences to make sense of and solve math problems?

4. How do your mathematics lessons provide opportunities for you to learn more about the multiple resources that students bring to the work of solving math problems?

Part 3

Rethinking Engagement with Families and Communities

Part 3 encourages teachers to reflect on the roles that parents and community organizations can play in deepening mathematics learning for students and reinforcing students' positive mathematics identities. Rethinking these roles may require additional effort. However, the benefits for classroom instruction, student engagement and learning, family participation, and community support are well worth the time.

Chapter 7 focuses attention on routine classroom interactions with parents about mathematics learning. Newsletters for parents and back-to-school night activities are modeled as ways to communicate a teacher's mathematics vision and showcase equity-based practices to help children learn mathematics. Specific communication strategies in the context of parent-teacher conferences are also modeled as ways to have a positive impact on students' identities. The chapter provides both conceptual and practical tools that can help teachers enlist parents to offer further support for children's mathematics learning and development.

Chapter 8 describes mathematics programs that partner with parents and community-based organizations to support mathematics learning *outside* the classroom. The chapter highlights two nationally recognized parent education programs—FAMILY MATH and MAPPS—which provide parents with tools and perspectives to support their child's mathematics education at home. An example also illustrates school partnerships with community and faith-based organizations to provide after-school mathematics support to students.

We encourage a paradigm shift in thinking regarding the roles and participation of parents and community organizations in a student's mathematics education. In-classroom and out-of-school examples can assist teachers in developing true partnerships with parents and community groups to support students' success in mathematics.

Chapter 7

Routine Practices to Engage Parents in Promoting Positive Math Learning and Identity

This chapter describes ways to enhance *routine teaching practices* by involving parents in supporting mathematics learning and positive mathematics identity development among students. Our goal in stressing equity-focused routine practices is to *enhance what you may already do*, as well as introduce a few new options that might offer you possibilities for increasing parent engagement and strengthening the teacher-parent relationship. We will focus on two types of routine classroom interactions with parents. First, we will explore common routines and events that many teachers use to introduce their mathematics practices to parents—specifically, classroom newsletters and "back-to-school night" events. Over the school year, these are likely to offer you your primary opportunities for communicating your vision of mathematics to parents and keeping them updated on the mathematics in your classroom. Second, we will examine classroom interactions related to mathematics progress and performance—namely, parent-teacher conferences. Conferences that involve the evaluation of children's mathematics progress and performance can create opportunities and challenges for teachers, parents, and students to positively shape mathematics learning and identity.

Enhancing communication practices that foster trust and mutual engagement among teachers, parents, and students to support math learning is key in equity-focused teacher practice (Adams and Christenson 2000; Christenson 2004; Minke and Anderson 2003). We believe that parents are underused resources as partners in mathematics learning and that building this partnership can greatly improve relationships between schools and the families that they serve.

Introducing Classroom Math Practices to Parents: Communicating Your Mathematics Vision

It is the beginning of the school year. You are getting your classroom ready, planning with your colleagues, reviewing your student lists, and preparing for the first day. You are outlining your goals, projects, and class management routines as you anticipate a new group of students. You are excited to meet your students and their families. Although all teachers develop welcome routines and practices designed to prepare students for the learning ahead, it is useful to take a closer look at specific classroom routines and practices that *introduce and welcome families to mathematics* in your classroom.

Think about how you communicate your vision for mathematics. What does mathematics learning looks like in your classroom? What will be taught, and how you will assess and support students? As discussed in chapter 3, your mathematics teaching identity—the totality of your beliefs and knowledge—shapes your mathematics vision and instructional practices. We now invite you to think carefully about how you share your vision for mathematics learning with your students' families when you employ two very common routine practices for parent-teacher communication: classroom newsletters and back-to-school nights. These are powerful tools for communicating your math vision to parents, and you can leverage them to support math learning and teaching in your classroom.

Classroom newsletters—showcasing mathematics

For many teachers, a common means of communicating with parents is the weekly classroom newsletter. The newsletter provides parents with important information about classroom activities and upcoming events. Often these newsletters have special sections that showcase specific subject areas, such as reading, science, music, and mathematics. We invite you to rethink your classroom newsletter to emphasize mathematics teaching and learning in two important ways. We suggest two actions. First, within the first month of school, send a newsletter devoted to your mathematics learning goals for the year. Second, prepare a monthly or quarterly newsletter devoted to what is happening in mathematics in the classroom. Frequent communication that chronicles mathematics activities and student successes will help keep parents informed and engaged in their students' mathematics learning.

To help with this process, we offer several design-related questions for mathematics newsletters:

- What is mathematics, and why is it important to learn?
- What are your goals for students as math learners?
- What does mathematics learning look like in your class?
- What does mathematics teaching look like in your class?
- How will you engage parents and the community in developing mathematics learning in your classroom?
- How will you help students with different mathematics preparation and levels of confidence succeed in mathematics?

- How will you help students with various ethnic, cultural, and socioeconomic backgrounds—some of whom are learning a second language—succeed in mathematics?

Below we discuss two examples of family newsletters that convey the teachers' mathematics vision for their classrooms. These samples are actual newsletters created by teachers whose real names appear in the discussion that follows. The first sample was sent to families of second graders early in the school year. The second sample was designed by a middle school mathematics teacher who sent out monthly math newsletters that focused on specific math topics. These newsletters offer examples of different ways to engage families as resources to support mathematics learning and positive identity development in the classroom. We consider these newsletters in turn in the discussion that follows.

Crazy for math

At the beginning of the school year, Mrs. Sabol, a new teacher working with second graders in an urban district in the Pacific Northwest, sent her students' families the two-page math newsletter shown in figure 7.1. Her school's student population is culturally diverse, with no identified racial or ethnic demographic group exceeding 30 percent. The school serves a sizeable population of English language learners (21 percent, compared with the state average of 8 percent), with the largest linguistic population speaking Spanish.

Mrs. Sabol's newsletter is informative and creative. She wants her students to be "crazy for math." Her newsletter positively conveys the equity-based mathematics teaching practices discussed in part 2 in many ways. It outlines very specific learning expectations that reflect a commitment to *going deep with mathematics*, *affirming mathematics learners' identities*, *leveraging multiple mathematical competencies*, and *challenging spaces of marginality*. On the newsletter's first page (fig. 7.1a) Mrs. Sabol conveys these expectations to parents and guardians:

Your child and I will be fellow travelers as we test ideas, make conjectures, develop reasons, and offer explanations.

We also will learn that:

- Every student brings knowledge to our classroom.

- Ideas are the currency of our classroom. Your child's ideas have the potential to contribute to everyone's learning, and will receive respect and response!

- Students must respect the need for everyone to understand their own methods and must recognize that there are often a variety of methods that will lead to a solution.

- Mistakes are an opportunity to learn. They give us a chance to examine errors in reasoning, and contribute to everyone's learning.

Dear Parents,

I am excited to have your child in my math class! I plan to encourage a spirit of inquiry, trust and expectation in my classroom.

Did you learn math from lectures and worksheets? Were you taught to simply repeat back what your math teacher told you? Were you then expected to apply these concepts in your real life?

Math has turned around!

We will link home and school in our math classroom by building on experiences your student shares with others in our class. I will teach your student to do math like they would in the real world, starting with problems, dilemmas and questions they would encounter in life! Your child and I will be fellow travelers as we test ideas, make conjectures, develop reasons, and offer explanations.

We also will learn that:
- Every student brings knowledge to our classroom.
- Ideas are the currency of our classroom. Your child's ideas have the potential to contribute to everyone's learning, and will receive respect and response!
- Students must respect the need for everyone to understand their own methods and must recognize that there are often a variety of methods that will lead to a solution.
- Mistakes are an opportunity to learn. They give us a chance to examine errors in reasoning, and contribute to everyone's learning.

*****My goal is to make your child crazy for math! Please complete the attached survey. With your help I can design math problems that connect with their life!*

Mathematically yours,

Mrs. Sabol

What is Math?

It is a science of concepts and processes that have a pattern of regularity and logical order.

Finding and exploring this regularity or order, and then making sense of it, is what doing mathematics is all about.

I Believe worthwhile math problems...

... allow for **connections** (to home and community)

... incorporate **multiple approaches and solutions** (using problem solving process and developing associated skills are often more important than the "right" answer).

... require **higher level thinking**

... facilitate **reasoning and communicating mathematically** (students need opportunities to talk about their math thinking).

Do you know?... "Researchers consistently find that the most important factor in school success is what they call "opportunity to learn."' If students are not given opportunities to learn challenging and high level work, then they do not achieve at high levels." -Jo Boaler (from What's Math Got to Do With It? Please see me if you would like the full article). Students in my classroom receive challenging, engaging, and high level work no matter what their confidence level.
My students work respectfully together and help each other!

(a)

Fig. 7.1. A math newsletter for families of Mrs. Sabol's second graders

Why is learning math so important?

We use math in every aspect of our lives in one manner or another. When we drive a car, we compute our speed and how many miles we have gone. We use math to balance checkbooks. Even musicians use math when playing instruments. You and your child use math when you:

- Go shopping
- Tip at restaurants
- Check the change you receive
- Measure ingredients
- Calculate time to do something
- Measure fabric to sew
- Read a clock
- Figure out batting averages
- Calculate mileage and gas money
- Buy lunch at school
- Divide pizza or other treats
- Measure weight
- Plan a lemonade stand
- Figure out the time somewhere else
- Calculate how many days until our birthday
- Play video games
- Measure distance
- Use a calendar
- Figure out the price of a sale item
- Decide when to set the alarm
- Use the telephone
- Count allowance
- Play board games
- Build something
- Calculate postage
- Figure out sales tax
- Watch football
- Budget money
- Read a thermometer
- Figure out cost of movie snacks
- Pay bills

Math Is Everywhere!

Help your child strengthen math abilities at home!

Everyday experiences at home can help your student learn math? Combining common sense with mathematical thinking helps your child learn! Look for times when math happens naturally.

For some ideas about finding math opportunities at home, → *visit: http://athomewithmath.terc.edu/* ←

(website available in Spanish and English)

Learning through problem solving:

- Puts the focus on ideas and sense making
- Develops math confidence
- Teaches students that math makes sense
- Provides a context to build meaning for concepts
- Allows an entry point for a wide range of students
- Provides valuable data to assist me in helping students and keep parents informed
- Allows for extensions and elaborations
- Reduces discipline problems
- Develops mathematical power
- Is a lot of fun!

My goals for your student:

Gain confidence and belief in abilities.

Be willing to take risks and to persevere

Enjoy doing math

To help your student reach these goals, I will:

Build in success!

Praise efforts and risk taking!

Listen to all students!

(b)

Fig. 7.1. A math newsletter for families of Mrs. Sabol's second graders, *continued*

Mrs. Sabol is setting the stage for her students and their families to understand the mathematics learning and teaching expectations of her classroom. She conveys the idea that math learning is a journey that she is making *with* her students. Ideas, reasoning, solutions, and mistakes are all part of the mathematics learning in this classroom. Student contributions are valued and respected. The last two sentences in the "Do you know?..." box at the foot of the first page (see fig. 7.1a) reiterate this idea:

Students in my classroom receive challenging, engaging, and high-level work no matter what their confidence level.

My students work respectfully together and help each other!

These statements suggest a strong commitment to building a mathematics learning community in which all students will actively participate, contribute, and learn. The statements emphasize mathematical proficiency and agency to support students' mathematics learning.

Mrs. Sabol's newsletter also makes explicit how to tap into students' *multiple resources of knowledge* and everyday experiences while affirming their cultural and linguistic knowledge. "Math is everywhere," the newsletter states, providing examples of the various ways that families use mathematics in common activities such as shopping, cooking, sewing, budgeting, and playing sports and video games. It also identifies a bilingual website (in English and Spanish; http://athomewithmath.terc.edu) where parents can find more ideas on math activities that families can do at home.

A noteworthy component of Mrs.Sabol's newsletter is an enclosed bilingual questionnaire (Spanish and English) for parents and families to complete to help Mrs. Sabol design meaningful and relevant mathematics lessons for her students (see fig. 7.2). She asks questions about family experiences, languages spoken, hobbies, traditions, work, and pets. The inviting tone of her statement about the questionnaire in the newsletter (*"With your help I can design math problems that connect with their life!"*) and her use of two languages welcomes parents as partners and resources in supporting mathematics learning and teaching in the classroom. Mrs. Sabol clearly intends to engage parents in helping students learn mathematics with her. She obviously wants to deepen her students' enjoyment of mathematics and assist them in seeing its relevance and connection to their world.

Make math come alive for your child!

Knowing about your child's background and knowledge will help me to design math problems that relate to their lives! Please complete this survey and return it to me as soon as possible. Help to make your student crazy about math!

1. Do you have a family pet or pets? If so, please list your pets and their names. _____
    _____
    If you do have pets, would you be willing to bring your pet for a visit to our classroom? _____
    _____
    _____

2. Does your child have experiences with grandparents or aunts and uncles who have interesting stories or experiences they could share with our class? _____
    _____
    _____

3. In what ways are you and your child proud of your home? Please use the space below to tell about your family's rituals and traditions including food, music, birthdays, holidays, and the work that family members do: _____
    _____
    _____
    _____
    _____
    _____
    _____
    _____

4. Do your family members share any hobbies?_____
    _____
    _____

5. What languages are spoken at home?_____

6. How many siblings does your child have? Brothers?_____   Sisters?_____

7. Volunteers are welcome and needed in our classroom! Do you or any other family member have time to contribute, or any interesting hobbies or activities you would like to share with our class? _____
    _____
    _____ If you
    would like to help out or share in our classroom, what is the best way to contact you?_____
    _____

Thank you for completing our survey!

Watch for news about how your child's experiences at home contribute to math problems in class!!

(a)

Fig. 7.2. A bilingual questionnaire in (a) English and (b) Spanish enclosed in Mrs. Sabol's newsletter to families

¡Haga que las matemáticas sean parte de la vida de su hijo/a!

Saber sobre las experiencias de su hijo/a me ayudará a diseñar lecciones de matemáticas que sean más pertinentes a su vida. Favor de contestar las preguntas abajo, y devuélva la encuesta lo más pronto que sea possible. Asi me ayudará a hacer que las matemáticas sean algo emocionante para su hijo/a.

1. ¿Ustedes tienen una mascota en la casa? Si es así, haga una lista de sus mascotas y sus nombres.

    _____.

    ¿Si ustedes tienen mascotas en la casa, estarían dispuestos a traerlos al salón de clases para una visita?_____

    _____

2. ¿Si hijo/a tiene abuelos o tíos/tías que podrían venir a nuestro salón a platicar con los estudiantes sobre sus experiencias? _____

    _____

    _____

3. Me gustaría aprender más de su familia. Utilice el espacio abajo para describir algunas de sus tradiciones importantes. Por ejemplo, cómo celebran los cumpleaños y días de fiesta, y cuál es la comida y la música que más les gusta. También describan los trabajos que hacen los miembros de la familia. _____

    _____

    _____

    _____

    _____

4. ¿Sus familiares tienen pasatiempos? Descríbalos aquí. _____

    _____

    _____

5. ¿Cuáles idiomas hablan en su casa? _____

6. ¿Cuántos hermanos/as tiene su hijo/a? ¿Hermanos?_____¿Hermanas?_____

7. Las personas voluntarias son totalmente bienvenidas en nuestro salón de clase. ¿Usted o algún miembro de su familia tiene tiempo para ayudar en la clase, o para platicar con los estudiantes de sus pasatiempos? _____
    _____¿Si a Ud. le gustaría ayudar en nuestro salón de clase, cuál es la mejor manera de contactarle?_____

    Gracias por contester estas preguntas.

    Esté atento a como las experiencias de su hijo/a contribuyen a las lecciones de matemáticas.

(b)

Fig. 7.2. A bilingual questionnaire in (a) English and (b) Spanish enclosed in Mrs. Sabol's newsletter to families, *continued*

The power of proportion

In middle school, mathematics learning can strengthen or diminish students' confidence in their ability to solve problems. "When am I ever going to use this?" is one of the most frequent questions raised by middle school students about mathematics. To preemptively address this common question, one middle school mathematics teacher, Ms. Le Sage, created a monthly mathematics newsletter for her students and their families, tied to specific math topics such as scale, ratio, and proportion.

An important feature of Ms. Le Sage's newsletter is a monthly calendar with scale-related mathematics problems and activities that families can investigate (see the sample in fig. 7.3). This monthly calendar feature complements the specific definitions, examples, and ways to solve problems involving ratio and proportion studied in the classroom. The newsletter gives parents and other adult caregivers an opportunity to learn in a variety of contexts.

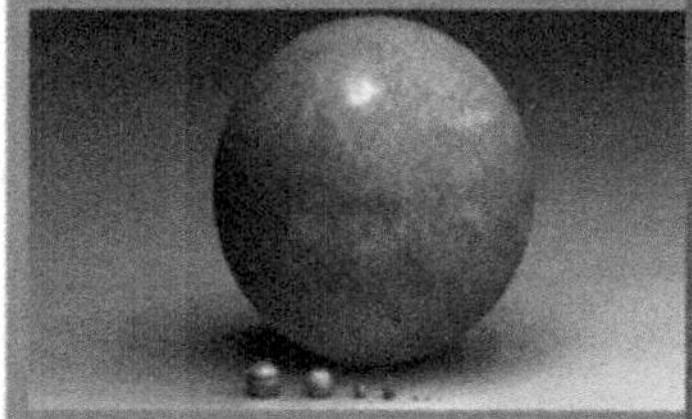

The picture shows a scaled model of the sun compared to other planets in the solar system.

January 2011

Sun	Mon	Tue	Wed	Thu	Fri	Sat
						1
2 Imagine if people were twice the size they are now.	3	4 Is 14% of 500 proportional to 14% of 5000? How about equal?	5 Play with Playdoh.	6	7	8 Make a batch of jello.
9	10 Start reading *The Borrowers.*	11	12	13 Use a map.	14	15 Make a larger scale 3:1 batch of jello.
16 Watch *Honey, I Shrunk the Kids.*	17 Play with legos.	18	19 Find a map that isn't drawn to scale. Is it still useful?	20	21 What kinds of things are measured in meters?	22 Draw your hand on a 2:1 scale.
23	24 What tools do you need to draw your home to scale?	25	26	27 Find Guam on a globe.	28	29 Draw two circles 1:4.
30 Which jobs use scale representations?	31					

Fig. 7.3. A sample calendar from a middle school teacher's monthly math newsletter

In the body of the newsletter (see fig. 7.4), Ms. Le Sage suggests various ways for families to engage in mathematics discussions that tap into their experiences and household funds of knowledge, encouraging them to use these as mathematics resources for deepening students' mathematical understanding (Civil 2007; Gonzalez et al. 2001). Family discussion prompts appear in the "Mealtime Moment" section of the newsletter, and specific questions in the "Project in Progress" section enable parents to ask their children about the class project currently under way—the restaurant project, which is related to scale and ratio and engages the students in floor plan design, recipe modifications, and seating arrangements.

January 2011

Miss Le Sage • 253-435-3000 Ext. 3142 • Desiree@leschischools.org

Math Beat

Big Time of the Math Dr. Wilfred Foster Denetclaw~ *Zoologist*

"My life has been shaped by the fairly traditional Navajo lifestyle I was raised in. It taught me to be respectful, and to be responsible...I did not do well my first time in college. I had been at the top of my class in high school, but I was not prepared for coursework at a major university. I had not learned how to write well and I did not have an understanding of mathematics or science that other students possessed. I did not know how to apply my time well for studying [or] how to use the educational resources at the university. I overcame these problems, first, by keeping my desire for a college education alive, second, by having my parents support my interest in college, and third, by getting serious about learning. Since, I have been involved in many interesting research projects... For example, I have been looking at the earliest stages of skeletal muscle development using the chicken embryo as a model for understanding muscle formation in humans."

Focus of the Week SCALE

Understanding scale is important because it engages proportional reasoning skills. Have you ever tried making a small batch of a recipe before cooking that recipe for a large group? You tested a small scale of the recipe! **Scales change the size of an entire representation by the same amount.** They can be used to plan, practice, or visualize for a variety of reasons. In NASA, scale models were often used because building a large scale spaceship incorrectly would be very costly. Scales save money! Helpful concepts in math scaling are multiplication, fractions, unit conversions (ex: feet to inches), and ratios.

Mealtime Moment

Why is it important for All the items on a map to be drawn to the same scale? What if you drew the roads on a different scale than city boundaries?

Scale is the ratio between the size of something and the representation of it.

Project in Progress

Currently, we are creating a scaled-down floor plan for our class restaurant that we have named _____. Ask your children questions about their design and bring up restaurant floor plans if you go out to eat! You can even talk about how your home dining area is set up. Then, we are going to discuss scaled-up recipes for making many servings of a single recipe. You can practice this one at home.

Algorithm Example

A model airplane is built on the scale of 1:18. If the wingspan of the plane is 30 feet, the wingspan of the model is how many inches?

Since the wingspan of the airplane was given to us in feet we must change it to inches. 30 feet = 360 inches.

Setting up the proportion:

$$\frac{model}{actual} = \frac{1}{18} = \frac{x}{360}$$

$$\frac{18x}{18} = \frac{360}{18}$$

x = 20 inches

Student Spotlight

_____ noticed that last year's yearbook used scale with some pictures, and didn't use scale with other pictures. She pointed out that the pictures that weren't scaled made people look different than what they really are. Great observation _____!

> What do YOU want your child to learn in math? I'd love for you to talk about your ideas for projects, lessons, field trips, guest speakers, etc. Never forget, you are an icon for your child.

Fig. 7.4. A math newsletter for families of middle school students

It is important to note that Ms. Le Sage teaches middle school mathematics at a tribal school. Tribal schools are independent schools run by Native American tribes for Native American students, to support cultural and linguistic sustainability of Native American heritage (some schools are affiliated with the Bureau of Indian Affairs and receive federal aid). One of Ms. Le Sage's goals is to connect her students and their families to Native American scientists. The newsletter features a biography of Wilfred Foster Denetclaw, Navajo and university biologist. Dr. Denetclaw offers advice on being educationally successful and discusses his research interests. Ms. Le Sage selected this biography to show a cultural role model in mathematics and science as a way to affirm her Native American students' mathematical identities. Although this may seem like a small connection, providing families with such examples produces additional sources of support to affirm students' multiple identities and continue their mathematics education. (Biographies of mathematicians and scientists of color are available from organizations such as the Society for the Advancement of Hispanics/Chicanos and Native Americans in Science [www.sacnas.org] and the Benjamin Banneker Association [www.bannekermath.org].)

Both of the sample newsletters that we have considered offer important resources to extend mathematics learning into family routines, enhancing opportunities to discuss mathematics with students at home. These are not typical "monitor homework" suggestions but authentic, creative ways to connect classroom mathematics learning with the students' home lives.

Curriculum back-to-school nights

Bringing parents and teachers together, the annual back-to-school night has become a hallmark of the school year. This common event offers teachers their primary opportunity to showcase for parents what their children will be learning during the school year. It is often the forum in which which teachers describe their learning expectations and curriculum foci. We encourage you to think about how you introduce your vision for mathematics to your parents at this event.

In the following vignette, the parent of a third grader at a public elementary school recounts her experience at back-to-school night. Her account suggests how a teacher's enthusiasm—or lack of enthusiasm—for a subject gets communicated to parents. Particularly noteworthy is how the teacher's presentation positions mathematics in relation to other school subjects:

We all sat at our child's desk, each family member (moms, dads, grandparents, sisters, aunts) eagerly wanting to know what was going to be learned. The teacher had a PowerPoint presentation projected on what she called the "smart board." The teacher enthusiastically described the new reading program ("in third grade we *read to learn* rather than *learn to read*"), the "fantastic" science projects (e.g., wetlands, solar system, salmon migration), and "really interesting" social studies projects (e.g., immigration and Native American history). However, when the slides turned to mathematics, the teacher's enthusiasm visibly waned as she gave the name of the curriculum used and gave the standardized testing dates and plans for test preparation. She spent less than a minute talking about math, with no examples and no smile. I wondered, does she even like teaching math?

The teacher's presentation exposes the limitations of her vision for mathematics. In contrast with her treatment of the other subjects, she discussed mathematics solely through references to the textbook and standardized tests, with no effort to highlight a set of mathematical competencies and relationships integral to students' problem solving or expanding ability to make sense of the world (Gutstein 2006; Schoenfeld 1992). The presentation did not associate mathematics with adjectives like "fantastic," "interesting," or "fun."

A key consideration for teachers about back-to-school night is the *image of mathematics* that is projected to families. Back-to-school night is an opportunity for you to clearly communicate the mathematical ideas and processes that students will be studying and why those topics are important. It is an opportunity to invite parents to participate in your mathematics vision for their children in new and exciting ways. Refining your message about your vision of mathematics as informative, creative, and positive can help set the stage for a positive year of mathematics learning. The following are some key elements to consider including in your back-to-school presentation about mathematics:

- Enthusiasm for the subject—communicating why math is important for students to learn (beyond being measured by standardized tests)
- Ways that you will nurture a positive math identity
- Ways that you will help strengthen students' mathematical proficiency and agency
- Your favorite mathematics topics to teach for this grade level and why you like these best
- The strengths of the mathematics curriculum and ways that you will enrich the students' mathematics experiences
- Special math projects (perhaps tied to science units or community service projects) that your students will do
- Ways that you will communicate your students' math progress to families
- Ways that parents can partner with you to support math learning (you might suggest family games—such as dominoes, chess or checkers, Parcheesi, cribbage, Connect Four, or spades—and you could actively point out ways that families can use mathematics in everyday events, such as estimating grocery bills, cooking, measuring fabric, completing repair projects)

To enrich this experience, you might consider distributing a mathematics survey to family members to obtain information that will help you to build on students' multiple knowledge bases and experiences. Like Mrs. Sabol's newsletter survey, your survey might give you information that you could use as another resource for your mathematics lesson planning. You might also distribute a mathematics resource list with activities and websites for families to visit after school or on weekends. Parents want to know how they can help their child to do well and enjoy learning mathematics. The key is to share your vision and how you want to work with the families to engage their children in mathematics learning that promotes a positive mathematics identity and gives them a strong mathematical knowledge base.

How Is My Child Doing in Math? Communicating Progress and Performance

Parents learn about their children's math performance in several other common ways, such as during parent-teacher conferences and through artifacts of performance—namely, report cards and unit and chapter assessments. These are *vulnerable contexts* for parents as they learn from another adult—an instructional expert—how their child is doing academically, socially, and emotionally. These interactions have the power to influence how parents will perceive a child's identity and success or failure in mathematics. Furthermore, these interactions introduce tensions and can create opportunities to increase or decrease trust between parents and schools (Adams and Christenson 2000; Christenson 2004; Minke 2003). Thus, the term *vulnerable* is fully warranted.

Consider the following scenario involving a Latina mother who recalled her recent parent-teacher conference about her third grade daughter, Xiomara:

The teacher began listing all her "weaknesses," from struggling with memorizing her addition, subtraction, and multiplication facts, to her inability to solve word problems. The teacher said that if Xiomara did not know her facts that she would be unable to solve more complex problems in fourth grade. The teacher showed examples of mistakes our daughter made on the most recent unit review test. Confused, I asked the teacher why she gave Xiomara a score of "3–meeting grade level standard" in mathematics on her most recent report card. The teacher responded by saying, "She seems to pull it together for the tests." I asked, "Is there anything Xiomara can do in math?" She simply said, "No. Xiomara really struggles." Then the teacher described all the "interventions" she gave our daughter during math lessons, such as extra tutoring from herself or a parent volunteer and extra time to complete assignments. We were unaware of this extra help that was being given to our daughter, and we asked why we had not been told earlier of her struggles since this was December. The teacher replied, "Don't you see the graded assignments and tests?" We walked away from this conference very upset. Our daughter had no mathematical strengths, only weaknesses. What does that mean? How can we help? There were no resources given to us.

According to the teacher, this child was not making adequate mathematical progress, even with several interventions. The teacher's intent was to bring this concern to the parents' attention during this critical school event—the parent-teacher conference. Unfortunately, the conflicting pieces of assessment data, the focus on the child's weaknesses, and the lack of direction to parents to help their child improve rendered this interaction very tense and unsupportive. The parents had now acquired a negative image of their daughter as a mathematics learner without being given any resources to address her needs.

Because parent-teacher conferences are critical venues for establishing and maintaining the trust required for effective school-family partnerships, it is essential to reflect on these interactions and their impact on parents' views of their children as mathematical learners. The images, evidence of progress, and mathematical strengths and needs that are communicated to parents can affect how they see their children as learners of mathematics and can shape at-home interactions with math.

To help facilitate productive and positive discussions about a child's mathematical progress and developing mathematics identity, we propose a basic template for parent-teacher conferences. The template, which appears in figure 7.5 (and is also available at nctm.org/more4u), communicates the core mathematics learning goals of a teacher's mathematics vision and reflects a holistic and balanced evaluation of a child's mathematics progress with a mathematics action plan (MAP) for learning support. The structure of the parent-teacher conference template reminds everyone that learning mathematics is important and that everyone can do it with encouragement and instructional assistance.

Parent-Teacher Conference Template

Math Vision: Your core mathematics learning goals, affirming why mathematics is important for children to learn (for example, working together to learn math together!). Every child can be successful in mathematics with the proper instruction, support, and encouragement.

Student: Teacher:

Mathematics Progress

Mathematics Strengths (Areas of Strength):

Mathematics Needs (Areas for Improvement):

Mathematics Action Plan (MAP)

Student Action:

Teacher Action:

Parent Action:

Fig. 7.5. A template for parent-teacher conference feedback

The template makes the child's mathematical strengths and needs explicit. Regardless of the grade on the report card, every child has mathematical strengths and needs. A child's mathematical strengths have to be affirmed for the child to maintain a positive mathematics identity. The student's mathematical needs must also be addressed for the student to move forward, developing mathematical knowledge and practices. Further, the MAP provides a space to record specific ways in which the student, parent, and teacher can work together to support and enrich the child's mathematics education.

We envision teachers using this parent-teacher conference template in conjunction with student work. Furthermore, the MAP should include a way that the student, teacher, and parent can address a specific need or build on a specific strength. For example, in the case of Xiomara, who is struggling with her addition, subtraction, and multiplication facts, the MAP might put following action items into place:

Student Action:

- Be positive. Remember, you can do this!

- Solve an online math puzzle or play an online math game. Check out "Primary Krypto" (http://illuminations.nctm.org/ActivityDetail.aspx?ID=173) or Calculation Nation's interactive game "Times Square" (http://calculationnation.nctm.org/Games/) to practice math facts.

- Spend 20 minutes three times a week practicing/playing the online game.

Teacher Action:

- Have Xiomara set up a hundreds chart to color-code facts that she knows. Talk with her about how to use these facts along with strategies like doubling to help her with facts that she is still working on.

- Set up a station lesson or menu lesson for students, with math facts as one of the required items. Other items might include math array games and patterns.

- Introduce *Number Talks* [Parrish 2010; structured ten- to fifteen-minute whole-class mental math discussions of number and operations] to reinforce skill with mental math and in decomposing numbers.

- Set up study groups for students to learn how to work and study together. Pair Xiomara with a student who has some efficient math strategies for multiplication facts.

Parent Action:

- Play online math games with Xiomara to practice math facts.

- Play family games like cribbage or dominoes to practice addition and multiplication.

- Work with Xiomara to create a "favorite number" book, with photographs, stories, and drawings representing Xiomara's favorite number in many different ways. Practice math facts with Xiomara by making calculations that use different numbers and operations to arrive at that number (Coates and Thompson 2003).

- Take a math walk or play "math I spy" at home, pointing out instances of multiplication arrays in the home, such as egg cartons, cupcake tins, window panes, candy boxes, shelves, and so on. Have Xiomara tell you the multiplication fact represented by the array.

Although the teacher should complete this template before the conference, part of it could be co-constructed by all participants during the meeting. For instance, the MAP can serve as a brainstorming tool and a memorandum of understanding for the student, teacher, and parent. Moreover, for older students, contributing ideas about how they will strengthen their own mathematics learning beyond the classroom door can be a way of supporting a sense of individual agency. The ultimate goal is to have everyone walk away from such a meeting with an understanding of the child's mathematical strengths and needs and a specific plan that shows how mathematics learning will be supported at school and home. We also encourage the teacher to follow up with parents and the student about progress on the action items. Communication with parents might be in the form of a quick e-mail or phone check-in to let them know how you have implemented your action items with their child. This contact can open up additional dialogues about progress or more support resources if needed.

Initially, creating a summary of strengths and needs and a MAP for each student will be time-consuming. However, we believe that the investment of this time will provide teachers with a deeper understanding of how to support each child more effectively, give parents and teachers alike concrete ways to affirm to the child that he or she can learn mathematics, and promote a culture of mutual trust and respect that can strengthen the teacher-parent partnerships that are needed to help children learn mathematics.

Conclusion

This chapter has examined some routine practices and contexts that allow teachers to communicate with parents about the mathematical learning environment in which their child participates. Although routine, these practices can be powerful in conveying mathematical ideas, learning goals, instructional strategies, and student progress.

Family newsletters and back-to-school nights can be tailored to promote a positive image of mathematics learning—an image that is exciting to both students and parents. This is important for two reasons: to combat the negative images that many adults have of mathematics and to provide clear direction and resources for families to connect with mathematics in new and inviting ways. In addition, these formats can also provide teachers with important information through surveys and conversations, and this information can be integrated into mathematics lessons to maximize interest, relevance, and participation.

Parent-teacher conferences are another regular practice with tremendous implications for how parents view their children as mathematical learners. The conference template that we have presented offers teachers a way to reaffirm their vision for mathematics learning in the classroom, engage in a more substantive discussion of a child's areas of mathematical strength and need, and give clear guidance through the mathematics action plan so that everyone—the child, the teacher, and the family member—can take responsibility for the child's mathematical learning. These kinds of actions can go a long way toward building families' trust in the teacher as a true partner, committed to helping their children learn mathematics with confidence.

DISCUSSION QUESTIONS

1. How do you communicate your math vision to families?

2. How do you communicate a child's mathematical strengths and needs to parents?

3. In light of the examples presented here, how might you strengthen your communication practices about mathematics with your families?

4. Think about a student who struggles or needs enrichment. What would a mathematics action plan (MAP) look like for that student?

Chapter 8

Partnering with Families and Communities to Support Children's Equitable Mathematics Learning

Parents—including all adult caregivers who play parental roles in children's lives, such as grandparents, guardians, foster parents, aunts, uncles, and so on—often underestimate the power of their words and actions on the children in their care:

> I didn't realize how much I was influencing my child's math performance by my comments that I was no good at math as a kid. I had to do something to change both of our attitudes. (EQUALS/FAMILY MATH parent)

It is well established that children whose parents are involved in their children's education experience higher academic achievement regardless of family income, level of education, or cultural background (Epstein 1996). This has also been shown to be true regarding their mathematics education (Desimone 1999; Epstein 1984; Yan and Lin 2005). However, engaging families—including parents and other adult caregivers—in ways that positively influence their children's mathematics learning can be challenging, given the content standards and accountability demands currently imposed on teachers and students. For example, federal requirements regarding student and school benchmarks for growth, along with the threat of state-imposed sanctions, have heightened scrutiny and control of classroom instruction, content, and pedagogy. Consequently, meeting district and state benchmarks consumes the majority of teachers' instructional planning time.

Furthermore, many parents and other adults have not experienced success in mathematics, a situation that can lead to math avoidance or anxiety that they unwittingly pass on to their children. These mathematics experiences can also prevent parents and caregivers from being involved in or advocating for their children's mathematics education. Parents who have experienced success in mathematics or who can afford to provide additional resources to enhance their child's mathematics learning are able to play a more active and influential role in their children's mathematics education (Martin 2000, 2006; Remillard and Jackson 2006). Consequently, their children may often feel more confident and competent in mathematics.

We believe that if teachers are to engage students who have been marginalized in mathematics education and increase their success, they must engage *all* parents in meaningful discussions about mathematics. Studies have shown that mathematics reform promotes a perspective on mathematics that is often unfamiliar and inaccessible to parents who have not had opportunities to learn mathematics in a conceptual way (see, for example, Remillard and Jackson [2006]). Furthermore, African American, Latina/o, and low-income parents often experience more challenges in relation to their children's education because they are frequently perceived as uncaring or disengaged (DeCastro-Ambrosetti and Cho 2005). They are often seen as obstacles rather than resources for their children and are subsequently left out of critical conversations about mathematics reform efforts and classroom instruction (Martin 2000, 2006; Peressini 1998; Remillard and Jackson 2006).

Creating and sustaining meaningful ways to interact with parents about their children's mathematical experiences in and out of school are paramount in helping children develop positive mathematics identities and achieve success in school. As discussed in chapter 7, school systems have established routines and structures, such as back-to-school nights, classroom newsletters, and parent-teacher conferences, to communicate with and, to a certain degree, partner with parents to enhance students' mathematics success. School systems and teachers, however, may need to forge new pathways and enlist parents' assistance in contexts beyond the classroom setting to achieve success with all students. Creating new pathways takes additional effort and time—both scarce commodities, given the demands of teaching and the complex lives of families. Making any change in one's teaching practice takes commitment and perseverance, but once new practices are internalized and the benefits become apparent, the practices become routine.

This chapter provides examples of parent-teacher partnerships focused on mathematics. The vignettes that follow demonstrate how partnering with parents and community groups from out-of-school settings can provide children with additional opportunities to deepen their conceptual understanding of mathematics and develop positive mathematics identities. We showcase the FAMILY MATH program (EQUALS, University of California, http://www.lawrencehallofscience.org/equals/aboutfm.html) and the Math and Parent Partners project (MAPPS, University of Arizona, http://mapps.math.arizona.edu) as models for parent engagement that transcend traditional school–home boundaries to create mathematically rich environments that can support mathematics instruction that occurs in classrooms.

We also discuss mathematics partnerships formed with community centers and faith-based organizations to provide additional ways to engage children in mathematics and affirm their mathematics identities. We invite teachers to reflect on their assumptions about parents, families, and communities and the roles that each plays in their

students' mathematical development and then consider how to connect those previous
assumptions with their new insights to enrich current partnerships and develop new
ones to engage families more fully as resources for mathematics teaching and learning.

Using Parent Mathematics Education Programs

Like Janelle's mother in the following dialogue, most parents want to help their children
succeed in mathematics:

> *Janelle:*   Mom, I'm done with my homework. Can I play a game on the
> computer?
>
> *Mom:*   Just a minute. Let me see your homework. You didn't finish,
> Janelle. What about the fraction problems?
>
> *Janelle:*   [*Sighs*] I got stuck on the last set of problems. Mrs. Schneider told
> us the rule. I know I need to make the bottom numbers the same.
> I just can't remember how.
>
> *Mom:*   It's OK. Let me show you another way to compare fractions.
> Remember the number-line activity we did during the FAMILY
> MATH night at school? You were good at showing me $^1/_2$ and $^1/_4$
> on the number line. Let's use that method to compare fractions in
> this problem.

Because Janelle's mother participated in a math program designed to assist parents in
helping their children at home, she now has the confidence, knowledge, and skills to
support Janelle's mathematics learning and can truly partner with her child's classroom
teacher. Many programs are designed to provide parents—particularly those whose
children have not achieved mathematical success—with the tools to help their child be
successful in mathematics.

The FAMILY MATH program

FAMILY MATH, an EQUALS program, is one of the earliest parent mathematics education programs. EQUALS is a mathematics and equity program based at the
Lawrence Hall of Science in Berkeley, California, focusing on creating access in mathematics for all students, particularly those who have been marginalized in mathematics education. FAMILY MATH focuses on providing *all* parents with the tools and
resources to support their children's mathematics education. At a site meeting, Virginia
Thompson, FAMILY MATH founding director, offered a description of the program:

Teachers who participated in our EQUALS workshops on mathematics and equity
wanted activities, other than worksheets, that they could give parents to help them
support their children's mathematics at home. Parents knew how to help their children increase their reading comprehension skills, even if they weren't avid readers
themselves. Reading at home was a comfortable, supportive interaction both parents
and children enjoyed. The context was not the same for mathematics.

The FAMILY MATH program helps parents and children learn mathematics together. A major goal of activities in the program is to create that same sense of routine enjoyment in mathematics activities that many families experience in reading activities and to help empower students mathematically by providing tools and resources that parents can use at home. Additional program goals include the following:

- Raise parents' awareness of the role that mathematics plays in their children's future

- Provide parents with strategies and materials to support their children's math learning at home

- Provide all parents with the understanding and tools to advocate for their children's math education

- Increase parents' conceptual understanding of mathematics content

FAMILY MATH format

FAMILY MATH activities focus on understanding key mathematics concepts in the context of a game or in an investigative format. These formats foster positive mathematics relationships between parents and their children. Parents are able to deepen their children's mathematics learning in a less formal context.

Consider, for example, a FAMILY MATH activity at the middle school level, "Let's Go to the Movies!" (Mayfield-Ingram and Ramirez 2005). This algebra activity is designed to help children practice combining like terms, a common algebraic procedure. The context of the activity is a school project: Century Hilltop Movie Theaters has invited students at Martin Luther King Middle School to preview twelve new "kid friendly" movies. The teachers want the students to write movie reviews, and they decide to sort the students into review groups by having them identify algebraic "like terms" ($6a^2b$, a^2b; $7xy$, xy; y^2, $-5y^2$). Each student receives a "movie ticket" with an algebraic term on it. At the FAMILY MATH class, each parent-child team sorts the movie tickets into like-term groups. The FAMILY MATH class leader models the process for sorting the term groups. She holds up two tickets and asks the teams to compare them. Are they for the same movie? How do the the team members know? How are the tickets alike or different? The family teams then work together to sort the tickets. Parents mimic the questioning strategies of the class leader, a technique that helps both parent and child develop inquiry habits of thinking for solving mathematics problems. These habits help parents assisting with homework at home as well as children working on classroom assignments at school.

This work with algebraic terms on movie tickets is preceded by an activity called "Do I Belong?" In this activity, families shuffle a set of cards showing algebraic terms such as $18b$, $18c$, x^2, $5x^2$, and $-12x^2$. They discuss whether the cards show the same variable and whether the exponent is raised to the same power. The FAMILY MATH leader facilitates a whole-group discussion about exponents. What does the number represent? How are $2x$ and x^2 different? The leader selects a family team to record the examples (such as $x + x = 2x$; $x \cdot x = x^2$) given by the group on poster board on a wall in the room (Mayfield-Ingram and Ramirez 2005).

These activities are designed to promote "math talk" among families to deepen student learning, support parent learning, and engage families in mathematical ideas.

Participating in these types of activities with a parent in a relaxed atmosphere provides more opportunities for a student to grapple conceptually with an important algebraic topic. It also enables parents to learn or reacquaint themselves with concepts so that they can help support their child's mathematics education.

In the FAMILY MATH class environment, it is not only acceptable but also required to ask questions, work together, and model different strategies. The classes are held in a variety of settings, including libraries, churches, and parent association meetings, and in a variety of time periods, such as Saturday mornings, early evenings, and summer and spring breaks. Moreover, most materials are translated into Spanish, Mandarin, and Swedish. Parents often team with teachers to facilitate classes that create an experiential bridge that they can cross and recross many times throughout the year to share information to support a child's mathematics understanding.

FAMILY MATH parent outcomes

By participating in FAMILY MATH classes, families can obtain the tools to address the tensions that they often see at home in their child's response to mathematics assignments. "I now see how my child thinks mathematically," is a typical comment from participating parents, who are then able to take this knowledge and apply it when working with their child at home, as in the following example, which involves fraction comparison and continues the dialogue at the beginning of the chapter between Janelle and her mother:

Mom:	OK. Janelle, we know they are fractions. Are they greater or less than 1?
Janelle:	Less than.
Mom:	How do you know?
Janelle:	Because the numerator is less than the denominator.
Mom:	Great! So how much of the number line do we need to draw?
Janelle:	[*Thinks a bit before responding*] Just the part from 0 to 1.
Mom:	Right. OK, let's draw some number lines.

Janelle's mother proceeded to draw number lines for each of the fractions. She started to draw the intervals but remembered the FAMILY MATH class discussion about the importance of letting children do the thinking for themselves. The parent's role is not to tell children *how to* but to help them *think through* what to do. So, instead, Janelle's mother handed her daughter the pencil to let her draw and label the fraction intervals. She asked, "How can you tell which one is the larger fraction?" Janelle responded, "The one that covers the most distance on the number line?" "Yes," her mother replied. "Why don't you finish the rest of the problems on your paper. Tomorrow, you can ask Ms. Schneider to show you the rule again for finding common denominators. It's helpful to know the rule also because it's sometimes quicker and more efficient than drawing a number line." Janelle said, "OK, but I'm glad you knew another way to solve the problems." Her mom responded, "Me, too. We can practice a few tomorrow night, using the rule."

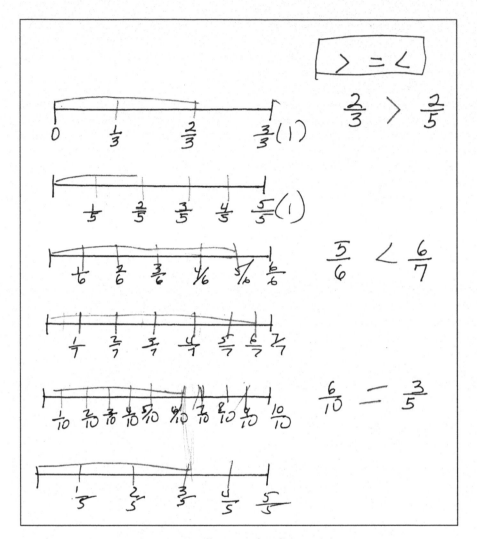

Fig. 8.1. Janelle's number line activity

These examples demonstrate how parent-child interactions can reinforce the equity-based practices that strengthen mathematics learning and support students' positive mathematics identities. For example, Janelle's mother was able to reinforce Janelle's conceptual understanding of a fraction as a number on a number line. Janelle could then use the structure to visualize and compare fractions. Teachers in earlier grades often use visual models to introduce fractions, and this was probably how Janelle encountered them earlier. In subsequent grades, however, many teachers rely on textbooks that quickly move to the standard algorithm for comparing fractions. Janelle's mother is tapping into previous mathematical knowledge of visual models of fractions to help Janelle make sense of these new fraction problems.

By using multiple representations—in this case, reconnecting Janelle to the visual model as another method to compare fractions—and encouraging Janelle to discuss the procedural rule with her mathematics teacher the following day, Janelle's mother helps to deepen her conceptual understanding of fractions. In this way, Janelle's mother is affirming her daughter's identity as a mathematics learner by helping Janelle practice perseverance with mathematics through coaching rather than explicitly doing the math problem for Janelle.

Allowing parents to experience standards-based mathematics tasks and activities can be much more beneficial than routine methods of disseminating mathematics reform to parents. This will become even more important with states' implementation of the Common Core State Standards for Mathematics (CCSSM; National Governors Association Center for Best Practices and Council of Chief State School Officers 2010). CCSSM is designed to increase student understanding and addresses both the content progressions necessary for student development and greater conceptual understanding. In addition to the Standards for Mathematical Content, CCSSM includes the Standards for Mathematical Practice, which identify the learning habits that students should exhibit as they engage in mathematical problem solving. These practices include learning to persevere, modeling with mathematics, and constructing viable arguments.

When a parent understands how and why teachers engage in instructional practices such as questioning to elicit children's thinking or using models or drawings to represent mathematical concepts, the family dialogue at home is transformed. The focus on "getting the right answer" is replaced by a focus on "helping my child understand the solution." Teachers have limited instructional time and many concepts to address. If we can provide additional avenues for students to engage in rich mathematics learning outside the classroom, we can create new opportunities for teachers to go deeper in developing concepts inside the classroom. Programs like FAMILY MATH can become important components in a teacher's mathematics program design.

Math and Parent Partners (MAPPS) project

Another program that creates partnerships between parents and teachers for student mathematics success is the Math and Parent Partners (MAPPS) project. Based on the funds of knowledge work in mathematics by Marta Civil and her colleagues, MAPPS explicitly rejects deficit views of families as lacking intellectual resources to help students learn mathematics. Instead, MAPPS views families as "intellectual assets" and seeks to support families in leveraging those assets by exploring concepts and skills that underlie the mathematics that children learn in kindergarten–grade 8 and connecting those concepts and skills with home and community activities (Civil and Andrade 2003; Civil and Bernier 2006). The program offers five minicourses (Thinking about Numbers; Thinking about Fractions, Decimals, and Percents; Geometry for Parents; Thinking in Patterns; and Data for Parents), spread out over a single semester and focusing on a mathematics theme.

Both parents and teachers take courses, together strengthening the parent-teacher relationship. The topics are presented through hands-on materials. Parents and teachers work in small groups and present their solutions to the whole group. Program evaluation has shown that teachers learn about parents' mathematical understandings, their problem-solving strategies, and their ways of explaining topics to their child. Teachers also gain mathematics knowledge for teaching and discover how to secure parent involvement in a way that enhances student learning. For their part, parents view their relationships with teachers in new ways, seeing themselves as equal partners in the mathematical development of their children. A Latina mother who co-facilitated parent workshops with teachers described this transformation:

It was hard in the beginning to work with the teachers. "They are the best." They don't give you the opportunity that you may know more or bring other ideas. Now we are more equal. Before [with her hands she indicates parents in the team were at a lower level than teachers], but now [she indicates they are at the same level]. Now they rely on me, they check with me, they make you feel that you are important to them. (Civil and Bernier 2006, p. 327)

The MAPPS program seeks to help parents and teachers work together to understand mathematics concepts and learn pedagogical strategies for communicating the content to children. After taking the minicourse Fractions, Decimals, and Percents, one parent commented on the newly gained content knowledge and how this knowledge would benefit the child (Knapp, Landers, and Jefferson 2012, p. 30):

Parent A: For example, one night we had this conversation: A half... what is the half of a quarter?

Interviewer: Oh?

Parent A: And would you believe that for years I didn't know what half of a quarter...

Interviewer: Half of a quarter.

Parent A: It is one-eighth.

Interviewer: Yes.

Parent A: And that you keep cutting it [*the fraction strip*] ... ummm ... $1/2$ of $1/8$ ...

Interviewer: So... you know. OK.

Parent A: And even on this test that I got... they asked me that question... $1/2$ of a quarter, and I could answer.

This parent learned conceptually that $1/2$ of $1/4$ is $1/8$ through a fraction-strip activity in the minicourse. Program evaluation has shown that parents gained content knowledge about turning percentages into fractions, calculating the volume of a cylinder, and raising a nonzero number to the zero power, obtaining 1 as the result. They also learned pedagogical strategies, such as using base-ten blocks or tangrams to assist their children in developing conceptual understanding related to number and geometry.

Participating teachers commented that they believed it was important for children to see their parents taking risks and persevering with mathematics. In addition, because teachers and parents shared instructional experiences, they were able to discuss the details and nuances of delivering mathematics instruction.

The MAPPS project creates avenues for teachers and parents to learn how to deepen a child's conceptual understanding of mathematics. Taking courses together allows teachers access to parents' multiple funds of knowledge. It also forges pathways between parents and teachers for continued discussions about mathematics teaching and learning strategies to support a child's mathematics identity, thus transforming parental involvement for parents and teachers alike, both of whom have powerful influences on a child's life. One parent described the gains from the program:

The point is to be part of the school and part of the community, just like a student. For me, the main part [of the MAPPS program] was parental involvement to use other parents to teach parents, I want to be part of that. (Civil and Bernier 2006, p. 328)

Partnering with Community Organizations

In addition to parent-teacher partnerships, community organizations can serve as instructional resources to support children's mathematical learning. In an attempt to support families, many community and faith-based organizations have established children's educational programs. They exist in local neighborhoods, making them closer and easier for families to use. This is particularly important when students cannot take advantage of before- or after-school supports or enrichment services.

This was the case for students attending Stuart Middle School, a California state-designated "distinguished school," known for its innovative instruction and high levels of student achievement. Stuart, a school in an urban district, is located in an upper-middle-class residential area that has recently experienced a demographic shift. As a result, the school draws an increasing number of students from the racially diverse and working-class "flatlands" communities in the district. Many of the flatlands students must get up at 5:30 in the morning and take several public and district buses to and from school each day.

The mathematics department at Stuart offers after-school tutoring and enrichment activities such as robotics. Unfortunately, if students don't live in the neighborhood or have someone to pick them up from school, they must take the district bus that leaves right after school. Because of bus schedules, the principal and staff had been unable to arrange for the students who live in the flatlands to take advantage of additional supports and enrichment programs. A teacher (identified as Pam in the exchange below) and a Title I community liaison (identified as Margaret) were talking about this problem in the faculty room during a recess break:

Margaret:	Hi, Pam. How are the parent conferences going? I saw your schedule on the door. Boy, you have a packed schedule.
Pam:	Yes, I have four more to go.
Margaret:	What's wrong? Are they not going well?
Pam:	No, they are all right, but I can't seem to get the parents of the kids I need to talk with to come to conferences. I sent several e-mails. Several of these students are way behind the other students in the class. They need more math support. Other students could really benefit from being on the robotics team. I tried to get them to attend the after-school sessions, but they have to catch the 3:15 bus.

Margaret: You know, until I had a child, I really didn't understand how much I was underutilizing a very powerful tool. Parents have busy lives and aren't always able to support their child in the ways schools select. You know, I think many of our parents attend First Congregational Church. The church has a tutorial and after-school center. There's also Taylor Baptist Church. I think I can get the phone number of each of the community directors. I know it's another step, but it is definitely worth the time if we can forge a partnership with these community churches.

In this case, the community liaison was able to meet with each director and set up meetings with the mathematics department chair, the principal, and the parent advisory council. The group decided to pursue a federal grant to provide professional development enabling church staff members to articulate connections between content offered during the regular school hours and that covered in out-of-school programs. The church staff members would also gain pedagogical content knowledge, allowing them to infuse mathematics strategies into their student educational programs. Margaret also planned to talk with the directors of the local Boys and Girls Clubs to determine whether they would like to join the partnership and perhaps sponsor a second meeting space for the robotics team. In the interim, the members of the group agreed to include one another on all mathematics-related correspondence with families regarding curriculum and assessment issues. Church and community directors were also granted access to the school's electronic newsletter and bulletins to increase community-home-school articulation.

Collaborating with church or community organizations can help teachers address student and family educational needs that the school system can't effectively tackle on its own. The mission of these community stakeholders is to support children and families so that they do not feel marginalized in their schools. Realizing the connection between mathematics success and a child's high school and college options, many of these stakeholders have directed their efforts to address educational access. Partnering with the faith-based and community resources in a child's life can provide teachers with opportunities to build on and deepen the mathematical development that they are trying to address in their mathematics programs. Furthermore, using the multiple resources in students' communities positively influences how they view themselves as mathematics learners and how they, in turn, are viewed by others in their communities.

Conclusion

A teacher must weave together many threads to create an environment in which each child feels and performs like a capable and confident mathematics student. Unfortunately, it isn't always easy to gather and tie together all the necessary threads. Parents and community groups are an underused resource for increasing students' mathematics proficiency.

Partnering with critical stakeholders can enable a teacher to implement many of the equitable practices stressed in this book, such as *going deep with mathematics, affirming mathematics learners' identities,* and *drawing on multiple resources of knowledge.* One of the inherent benefits of any partnership is that its members bring different resources to the table, and, by pooling these, all parties can secure what they need to reach their mutual goals. Teachers, parents, and community stakeholders clearly have a common goal: increasing students' mathematics success.

DISCUSSION QUESTIONS

1. How would you describe your parents' level of support for their children's mathematics education? What evidence contributes to your description?

2. How would you describe your parents' level of participation in their children's mathematics education in school and out of school? What evidence contributes to your description? What would you like to change or stay the same?

3. What resources at your school are available to families who want additional knowledge or strategies to support their children's mathematics instruction?

4. What community organizations could you partner with, or what community resources could you use, to secure further support for students in your classroom?

Walking the Path toward Equity

We hope that this book has intensified your commitment to helping children become powerful learners and doers of mathematics. We also hope that it has strengthened your conviction that developing positive mathematics identities is an important—and achievable—goal. Our primary message throughout this book has been that empowering students in mathematics requires deep reflection on the role of mathematics in students' lives. One critical aspect of your deeper reflection and developing equity-based practice is learning about the backgrounds and multiple identities of your students, how those identities emerge in school and nonschool contexts, your own influence on those identities, and how those identities influence the variety of ways in which students engage with mathematics. These identities should not be reduced to stereotypes.

We have also invited you to reflect on your own personal and professional identities to understand the impact of those experiences on your own identity in relationship to mathematics and your instructional practices. As you reflect, you may discover or rediscover that your own experiences as a mathematics learner have shaped your interactions with students and mathematics content. Moreover, you may confirm that, like your students, your views of yourself as a learner and doer of mathematics—your math identity—intersects with other important identities that you have developed.

The five equity-based practices discussed in this book—going deep with mathematics, leveraging multiple mathematical competencies, affirming mathematics learners' identities, challenging the spaces of marginality, and drawing on multiple resources of knowledge—highlight ways that you can strengthen students' mathematics learning and mathematics identities. You may find that assessing your own practice in relation to these practices will be a positive first step. Or you may have already incorporated aspects of these practices. Using the conceptual tools and practical examples provided in this book may help you to revisit, rethink, or recommit to your practice.

We acknowledge that changing one's practice takes time. Yet, the need to do so has an urgency that must be taken seriously if we want to see growth in children's mathematical development—particularly among those children who have historically had the least access to and success in mathematics.

Another critical avenue for engaging in equity-based practices is through assessment. Reflecting on the ways in which you communicate math progress to your students and, by extension, their parents, is key. The models of meaningful feedback provided in this book offer ways to focus students' attention on making sense of mathematics at their current levels of understanding. Traditional feedback, offered to students through check marks, tallies of correct answers, or smiley faces, communicates little to them about how to improve. Grading papers is a routine practice; rethinking how you give feedback to provide information that can strengthen learning and affirm a positive mathematics identity is an equity-based assessment practice that takes time but is worth the investment to help students make progress in mathematics.

Because you are not alone in your support of children's mathematics learning, we have also asked you to reflect on the kinds of parent, family, and community engagement practices that you use to support mathematics learning and teaching in your classroom. Routine practices like classroom newsletters and curriculum night events provide opportunities for you to convey your math vision to parents. These can also be opportunities for you to get to know families as potential resources for your mathematics lessons. By communicating your vision of mathematics teaching and learning in ways that convey a positive, enthusiastic view of mathematics and a confidence in *all* students' ability to learn, you can help initiate a strong partnership to help support mathematics learning in the classroom.

We hope that you share our position that parents and communities can be important resources for supporting children's mathematics learning. FAMILY MATH and Math and Parent Partners (MAPPS), highlighted in chapter 8, are just two examples of programs that support children and families in mathematics. We encourage you to learn about these and similar programs. Furthermore, partnering with faith-based and community organizations can also foster positive partnerships that support children's mathematical development.

Critical reflection on the various ways in which mathematics learning, teaching, and identity are interlinked takes commitment and time. Taking action to change one's instructional practice to accommodate this new knowledge requires courage and perseverance. Changing habits of thinking and pedagogical frameworks may seem artificial or cumbersome at first, but the new practices gradually become easier and more natural. What every teacher wants is to engage and support students to be confident and competent mathematical problem solvers. What we have tried to outline in this book are strategies and perspectives that support this goal and are based on research and our collective experiences as mathematics educators.

Further, it has been our aim to make these equity-based practices more transparent by offering examples that will resonate as true and realistic, enabling teachers to see themselves, the students that they teach, and the parents and community that they serve as partners on a journey toward mathematics success. Many teachers are already on this path, and we hope that you have gained knowledge to support and enhance your efforts. You may now have a clearer sense of what equity-based elements create a classroom that strengthens children's mathematics learning and identities.

There are many ways to make progress on the path toward equity. It is important to understand that the work of achieving equity is never finished. It is a journey. Different entry points provide opportunities to make progress in various ways but not all at once. The equity-based strategies that you initiate should be connected to your professional goals and teaching vision.

We encourage you to take steps along this path. One possible first step might be to write your own math autobiography, detailing how your own experiences and identities were shaped, enabling you to reflect on how your personal history might influence how you teach mathematics. A second step might be to focus on assessment that gives students feedback to move their mathematical thinking forward instead of simply giving them a grade on their work. A third step might be to focus on how you communicate with parents about your vision for mathematics.

Furthermore, a vital step is to involve your colleagues in this process. We would encourage you to connect with other colleagues at your school site to reflect on the information in this book. Select a chapter to read together and use the questions at the end to guide your discussion. Implementing equity-based practices is doable, with many different places to begin. However, we must take action. Too many of our children never have the chance to know the power of a strong mathematics education. We all must take steps forward to make progress on this path.

References

Adams, Kimberly S., and Sandra L. Christenson. "Trust and the Family-School Relationship: Examination of Parent-Teacher Differences in Elementary and Secondary Grades." *Journal of School Psychology* 38, no. 5 (2000): 477–97.

Aguirre, Julia. "Privileging Mathematics and Equity in Teacher Education: Framework, Counter-Resistance Strategies and Reflections from a Latina Mathematics Educator." In *Culturally Responsive Mathematics Education*, edited by Brian Greer, Swapna Mukhopadhyay, Arthur B. Powell, and Sharon Nelson-Barber, pp. 295–319. New York: Routledge, 2009.

Aguirre, Julia M., Erin E. Turner, Tonya Gau Bartell, Corey Drake, Mary Q. Foote, and Amy Roth McDuffie. "Analyzing Effective Mathematics Lessons for English Learners: A Multiple Mathematical Lens Approach." In *Beyond Good Teaching: Advancing Mathematics Education for ELLs,* edited by Sylvia Celedón-Pattichis and Nora Ramirez, pp. 207–22. Reston, Va.: National Council of Teachers of Mathematics, 2012.

Ashlock, Robert B. *Error Patterns in Computation: Using Error Patterns to Improve Instruction.* Upper Saddle River, N.J.: Pearson, 2002.

Beijaard, Douwe, Paulien C. Meijer, and Nico Verloop. "Reconsidering Research on Teachers' Professional Identity." *Teaching and Teacher Education* 20, no. 2 (2004): 107–28.

Berry, Robert Q., III. "Access to Upper-Level Mathematics: The Stories of African American Middle School Boys Who Are Successful with School Mathematics." *Journal for Research in Mathematics Education* 39 (2008): 464–88.

Black, Paul, Christine Harrison, Clare Lee, Bethan Marshall, and Dylan Wiliam. "Working Inside the Black Box: Assessment for Learning in the Classroom." *Phi Delta Kappan* 86, no. 1 (2004): 9–21.

Blum-Anderson, Judy. "Increasing Enrollment in Higher-Level Mathematics Classes through the Affective Domain." School Science and Mathematics 92, no. 8 (1992): 433–36.

Boaler, Jo. *Experiencing School Mathematics: Traditional and Reform Approaches to Teaching and Their Impact on Student Learning.* Rev. ed. Mahwah, N.J.: Lawrence Erlbaum, 2002.

———. *What's Math Got to Do with It? Helping Children Learn to Love Their Least Favorite Subject—and Why It's Important for America.* New York: Viking, 2008.

Brenner, Mary E., and Judit N. Moschkovich. "Everyday and Academic Mathematics in the Classroom." *Journal for Research in Mathematics Education* Monograph 11. Reston, Va.: NCTM, 2002.

Christenson, Sandra L. "The Family-School Partnership: An Opportunity to Promote the Learning Competence of All Students." *School Psychology Review* 33, no. 1 (2004): 83–104.

Civil, Marta. "Building on Community Knowledge: An Avenue to Equity in Mathematics Education." In *Improving Access to Mathematics: Diversity and*

Equity in the Classroom, edited by Na'ilah Suad Nasir and Paul Cobb, pp. 105–17. New York: Teachers College Press, 2007.

Civil, Marta, and Rosi Andrade. "Collaborative Practice with Parents: The Role of the Researcher as Mediator." In *Collaboration in Teacher Education: Examples from the Context of Mathematics Education,* edited by Andrea Peter-Koop, Vânia Santos-Wagner, C. J. Breen, and A. J. C. Begg, pp. 153–68. Dordrecht, The Netherlands: Kluwer, 2003.

Civil, Marta, and Emily Bernier. "Exploring Images of Parental Participation in Mathematics Education: Challenges and Possibilities." *Mathematical Thinking and Learning* 8, no. 3 (2006): 309–30.

Coates, Grace Dávila, and Virginia Thompson. *Family Math II: Achieving Success in Mathematics, K–6.* Berkeley, Calif.: Lawrence Hall of Science, 2003.

Cornell, Stephen E., and Douglas Hartmann. *Ethnicity and Race: Making Identities in a Changing World.* Thousand Oaks, Calif.: Pine Forge Press, 1998.

DeCastro-Ambrosetti, Debra, and Grace Cho. "Do Parents Value Education? Teachers' Perceptions of Minority Parents." *Multicultural Education* 13, no. 2 (2005): 44–46.

Desimone, Laura. "Linking Parent Involvement with Student Achievement: Do Race and Income Matter?" *Journal of Educational Research* 93, September/October 1999, 11–30.

Dorner, Lisa M., Marjorie Faulstich Orellana, and Christine P. Li Grining. "'I Helped My Mom,' and It Helped Me: Translating the Skills of Language Brokers into Improved Standardized Test Scores." *American Journal of Education* 113, no. 3 (2007): 451–78.

Drake, Corey, James P. Spillane, and Kimberly Hufferd-Ackles. "Storied Identities: Teacher Learning and Subject-Matter Context." *Journal of Curriculum Studies* 33, no. 1 (2011): 1–23.

Epstein, Joyce. "Effects of Teacher Practices of Parent Involvement Change in Student Achievement in Reading and Math." Paper presented at the Annual Meeting of the American Educational Research Association, New Orleans, La., April 23–27, 1984.

——. "Advances in Family, Community, and School Partnerships." *Community Education Journal* 23, no. 3 (1996): 10–15.

EQUALS/FAMILY MATH. Lawrence Hall of Science, University of California at Berkeley. http://www.lawrencehallofscience.org/equals.

Featherstone, Heather, Sandra Crespo, Lisa M. Jilk, Joy A. Oslund, Amy Noelle Parks, and Marcy B. Wood. *Smarter Together! Collaboration and Equity in the Elementary Math Classroom.* Reston, Va.: National Council of Teachers of Mathematics, 2011.

González, Norma, Rosi Andrade, Marta Civil, and Luis C. Moll. "Bridging Funds of Distributed Knowledge: Creating Zones of Practices in Mathematics." *Journal of Education for Students Placed at Risk* 6, nos. 1–2 (2001): 115–32.

Gresalfi, Melissa Sommerfeld, and Paul Cobb. "Negotiating Identities for Mathematics Teaching in the Context of Professional Development." *Journal of Mathematics Education* 42, no. 3 (2011): 270–304.

Gresalfi, Melissa S., Taylor Martin, Victoria Hand, and James Greeno. "Constructing Competence: An Analysis of Student Participation in the Activity

Systems of Mathematics Classrooms." *Educational Studies in Mathematics* 70, no. 1 (2009): 49–70.

Gutiérrez, Rochelle. "Beyond Essentialism: The Complexity of Language in Teaching Mathematics to Latina/o Students." *American Educational Research Journal* 39, no. 4 (2002): 1047–88.

———. "The Sociopolitical Turn in Mathematics Education." *Journal for Research in Mathematics Education* 4, no. 0 (*JRME* Equity Special Issue) (2010): 1–32.

Gutstein, Eric. *Reading and Writing the World with Mathematics: Toward a Pedagogy for Social Justice*. New York: Routledge, 2006.

Gutstein, Eric, and Bill Petersen. *Rethinking Mathematics: Teaching Social Justice by the Numbers*. Milwaukee, Wis.: Rethinking Schools, 2005.

Horn, Ilana. *Strength in Numbers: Collaborative Learning in Secondary Mathematics*. Reston, Va.: National Council of Teachers of Mathematics, 2012.

Hurtado, Aída, and Patricia Gurin. *Chicana/o Identity in a Changing U.S. Society: Quién Soy? Quiénes Somos?* Tucson: University of Arizona Press, 2004.

Jackson, Kara. "The Social Construction of Youth and Mathematics: The Case of a Fifth-Grade Classroom." In *Mathematics Teaching, Learning, and Liberation in the Lives of Black Children*, edited by Danny Bernard Martin, pp. 175–99. New York: Routledge, 2009.

Knapp, Andrea, Rachel Landers, and Vetrece Jefferson. *Research Report on Parents and Children in MAAPS*. Athens, Ga.: University of Georgia, 2012.

Kuhs, Therese M., and Deborah L. Ball. "Approaches to Teaching Mathematics: Mapping the Domains of Knowledge, Skills, and Dispositions." Unpublished manuscript, National Center for Teacher Education, Michigan State University, 1986. http://staff.lib.msu.edu/corby/education/Approaches _to_Teaching_Mathematics.pdf.

Lampert, Magdalene. *Teaching Problems and the Problems of Teaching*. New Haven, Conn.: Yale University Press, 2001.

Lee, Stacey J. *Up Against Whiteness: Race, School, and Immigrant Youth*. New York: Teachers College Press, 2005.

———. *Unraveling the "Model Minority" Stereotype: Listening to Asian American Youth*. 2nd ed. New York: Teachers College Press, 2009.

Louie, Vivian. *Compelled to Excel: Immigration, Education, and Opportunity among Chinese Americans*. Palo Alto, Calif.: Stanford University Press, 2004.

Manyak, Patrick C. "'What Did She Say?': Translation in a Primary-Grade English Immersion Class." *Multicultural Perspectives* 6, no. 1 (2004): 12–18.

Martin, Danny B. *Mathematics Success and Failure among African American Youth: The Roles of Sociohistorical Context, Community Forces, School Influence, and Individual Agency*. Mahwah, N.J.: Lawrence Erlbaum, 2000.

———. "Mathematics Learning and Participation as Racialized Forms of Experiences: African-American Parents Speak on the Struggle for Mathematics Literacy." *Mathematical Thinking & Learning* 8, no. 3 (2006): 197–229.

———. "Liberating the Production of Knowledge about African American Children and Mathematics." In *Mathematics Teaching, Learning, and Liberation in* the Lives of Black Children, edited by Danny Bernard Martin, pp. 3–36. New York: Routledge, 2009.

Math and Parent Partners (MAPPS). University of Arizona. http://mapps.math. arizona.edu.

Mathematics Assessment Resource Service (MARS). Silicon Valley Mathematics Initiative, 2010. http://www.svmimac.org/home.html.

Mayfield-Ingram, Karen, and Alma Ramirez. The Journey—Through Middle School Math. Berkeley, Calif.: EQUALS Programs, Lawrence Hall of Science, University of California at Berkeley, 2005.

Miller-Jones, Dalton, and Brian Greer. "Conceptions of Assessment of Mathematical Proficiency and Their Implications for Cultural Diversity." In Culturally Responsive Mathematics Education, edited by Brian Greer, Swapna Mukhopadhyay, Arthur B. Powell, and Sharon Nelson-Barber, 165–86. New York: Routledge, 2009.

Minke, Kathleen M., and Kellie J. Anderson. "Restructuring Routine Parent-Teacher Conferences: The Family-School Conference Model." Elementary School Journal 104, no. 1 (2003): 49–69.

Moschovich, Judit N. "Learning Mathematics in Two Languages: Moving from Obstacles to Resources." In Changing the Faces of Mathematics: Perspectives on Multiculturalism and Gender Equity, edited by Walter Secada, pp. 85–93. Reston, Va.: National Council of Teachers of Mathematics, 1999.

————. "A Situated and Sociocultural Perspective on Bilingual Mathematics Learners." Mathematical Thinking and Learning 4, nos. 2–3 (2002): 189–212.

National Council of Teachers of Mathematics (NCTM). Assessment Standards for School Mathematics. Reston, Va.: NCTM, 1995.

National Governors Association Center for Best Practices and Council of Chief State School Officers (NGA Center and CCSSO). Common Core State Standards (College- and Career-Readiness Standards and K–12 Standards in English Language Arts and Math). Washington, D.C.: NGA Center and CCSSO, 2010. http://www.corestandards.org.

National Research Council. Adding It Up: Helping Children Learn Mathematics. Mathematics Learning Study Committee, Jeremy Kilpatrick, Jane Swafford, and Bradford Findell, eds. Center for Education, Division of Behavioral and Social Sciences and Education. Washington, D.C.: National Academy Press, 2001a.

————. Improving Mathematics Education: Resources for Decision Making. Committee on Decisions That Count, Steve Leinwand and Gail Burrill, eds. Mathematical Sciences Education Board, Center for Education, Division of Behavioral and Social Sciences and Education. Washington, D.C.: National Academy Press, 2001b.

Oakes, Jeannie. Keeping Track: How Schools Structure Inequality. 2nd ed. New Haven, Conn.: Yale University Press, 2005.

Olsen, Brad. "'I Am Large, I Contain Multitudes': Teacher Identity as a Useful Frame for Research, Practice, and Diversity in Teacher Education." In Studying Diversity in Teacher Education, edited by Arnetha F. Ball and Cynthia A. Tyson, pp. 257–73. Lanham, Md.: Rowman & Littlefield, 2011.

Orellana, Marjorie Faulstich. *Translating Childhoods: Immigrant Youth, Language, and Culture.* Piscataway, N.J.: Rutgers University Press, 2009.

Parrish, Sherry D. *Number Talks: Helping Children Build Mental Math and Computation Strategies, Grades K-5.* Sausalito, Calif.: Math Solutions, 2010.

Peressini, Dominic D. "The Portrayal of Parents in the School Mathematics Reform Literature: Locating the Context for Parental Involvement." *Journal for Research in Mathematics Education* 29 (1998): 555–82.

Remillard, Janine T., and Kara Jackson. "Old Math, New Math: Parents' Experiences with Standards-Based Reform." *Mathematical Thinking & Learning* 8, no. 3 (2006): 231–59.

Russell, Susan Jo. "Developing Computational Fluency with Whole Numbers." *Teaching Children Mathematics* 7, no. 3 (2000): 154–58.

Schoenfeld, Alan H. "Learning to Think Mathematically: Problem Solving, Metacognition, and Sense Making in Mathematics." In *Handbook of Research on Mathematics Teaching and Learning*, edited by Douglas A. Grouws, pp. 334–70. New York: Macmillan; Reston, Va.: National Council of Teachers of Mathematics, 1992.

Simic-Muller, Ksenjia, Erin E. Turner, and Maura C. Varley. "Math Club Problem-Posing." *Teaching Children Mathematics* 16, no. 4 (2009): 206–12.

Spielhagen, Frances R. *The Algebra Solution to Mathematics Reform: Completing the Equation.* New York: Teachers College Press, 2011.

Staats, Susan. "Somali Mathematics Terminology: A Community Exploration of Mathematics and Culture." In *Multilingualism in Mathematics Classrooms: Global Perspectives*, edited by Richard Barwell, pp. 32–46. Bristol, Conn.: Multilingual Matters, 2009.

Stein, Mary Kay, Margaret Schwan Smith, Marjorie A. Henningsen, and Edward A. Silver. *Implementing Standards-Based Mathematics Instruction: A Casebook for Professional Development.* New York: Teachers College Press, 2000.

Stinson, David. "Negotiating Sociocultural Discourses: The Counter-Storytelling of Academically (and Mathematically) Successful African American Male Students." *American Educational Research Journal* 45, no. 4 (2008): 975–1010.

Stipek, Deborah, Karen B. Givvin, Julie M. Salmon, and Valanne L. MacGyvers. "Teacher Beliefs and Practices Related to Mathematics Instruction." *Teaching and Teacher Education* 17 (February 2001): 213–26.

Tate, William F. "Race, Retrenchment, and Reform of School Mathematics." *Phi Delta Kappan* 75, no. 6 (1994): 477–84.

Turner, Erin. "Critical Mathematical Agency: Urban Middle School Students Engage in Significant Mathematics to Understand, Critique, and Act upon Their World." PhD diss., University of Texas, 2003.

Turner, Erin E., Corey Drake, Amy Roth McDuffie, Julia M. Aguirre, Tonya Gau Bartell, and Mary Q. Foote. "Promoting Equity in Mathematics Teacher Preparation: A Framework for Advancing Teacher Learning of Children's Multiple Mathematics Knowledge Bases." *Journal of Mathematics Teacher Education* 15, no. 1 (2012): 67–82.

Turner, Erin E., and Beatriz T. Font Strawhun. "Posing Problems That Matter: Investigating School Overcrowding." *Teaching Children Mathematics* 13, no. 9 (2007): 457–63.

Turner, Erin, and Sylvia Celedón-Pattichis. "Problem Solving and Mathematical Discourse among Latino/a Kindergarten Students: An Analysis of Opportunities to Learn." *Journal of Latinos and Education* 10, no. 2 (2011): 146–69.

University of Chicago School Mathematics Project. Everyday Mathematics. Chicago: McGraw Hill, 2007.

Yan, Wenfan, and Qiuyun Lin. "Parent Involvement and Mathematics Achievement: Contrast across Racial and Ethnic Groups." *Journal of Educational Research* 99, no. 2 (2005): 116.